A Pocket Guide to
Literature and Language Terms

By

Benjamin W. Griffith
Dean, The Graduate School
West Georgia College

Over 500 Terms and Expressions Used in Writing
Guides, Literary Journals, and Classroom Discussions

Composition	Literature
Grammar	Punctuation
Language	Sentence Structure

New York • London • Toronto • Sydney

All inquires should be addressed to:
Barron's Educational Series, Inc.
250 Wireless Boulevard
Hauppauge, New York 11788

Library of Congress Catalog Card No. 85-13451

International Standard Book No. 0-8120-2512-1

Library of Congress Cataloging in Publication Data

Griffith, Benjamin W.
  Pocket guide to literature and language terms.

  Includes index.
  1. Philology—Terminology. I. Title.
P29.5.G74 1985   401'.14   85-13451
ISBN 0-8120-2512-1

PRINTED IN THE UNITED STATES OF
AMERICA

   7   9 8 7 6 5 4 3 2

CONTENTS

Introduction: How to Use This Book

INTRODUCTION

From the first grade through college, students take courses which are ambiguously called "English" courses. No courses are more varied in scope than those that are placed in the mixed bag called "English." They deal at various times with terms relating to literary criticism, to the forms and structure of literature, to figures of speech, to grammar and language, to punctuation, to composition and writing, to logic and the techniques of persuasion, and even to philosophy. It is the purpose of this book to provide a compact reference tool that will give students brief definitions, along with examples, of terms they are likely to encounter in their courses. Good communication between teacher and student or textbook and student depends on a mutual understanding of the basic terms, and it is hoped that this book will increase that understanding.

This glossary of specialized terms used in English courses is divided into two principal parts. The first defines terms one might use in the study of literature, and the second part defines terms used in courses that teach grammar and composition. A few words, like "apostrophe," are found in both parts, with completely different meanings. If one read the book from cover to cover, it would be noticed that some terms recur with different names, yet each is separately, though similarly, defined. Perhaps it is a personal foible of the author, but he dislikes looking up a term such as

"aphorism," only to be told to "See EPIGRAM." The
definitions and examples are brief, allowing the author to make each one self-contained and to avoid
sending the reader scurrying through the pages on a
chase. Cross references are provided merely to show
similar terms.

Some of the terms, such as "existentialism," are pro-
found in their implications and difficult to define in a
narrow scope. The reader should be warned that definitions of such philosophical terms are far from complete.
The author's definitions can only establish a basis for
an understanding that can emerge fully when the student has read widely in the literature and absorbed the
meaning by long immersion in the idea.

Anyone who writes such a book as this must acknowl-
edge a debt to the excellent reference books that have
come before, particularly Thrall, Hibbard, and Hol-
man, *A Handbook of Literature* (Third edition, 1980),
and Harry Shaw's *Dictionary of Literary Terms* (1972).
I am also indebted to Professor Donald J. Gray for his
suggestions, which greatly improved the first draft of
this book. He is not to be blamed, of course, for any of
the imperfections that may still remain.

PART I
LITERARY
TERMS

abstract poetry Poetry that uses words for their sound qualities rather than for their meaning. Like abstract painting, which uses colors and shapes to convey meaning but represents no specific objects, abstract poetry does not attempt to convey meaning in the traditional sense.

EXAMPLE: *The Pterodactyl made its nest*
And laid a steel egg in her breast—
Under the Judas-colored sun.
                    Dame Edith Sitwell

Absurd, the Literature or drama that has as its basic premise the meaninglessness of life in the 20th century, where man is separated from his religious and philosophical roots and therefore lives in isolation in an alien world. Works that depict the absurd use nightmarish fantasy, inconsistencies, and even banal repetitions to suggest the absurdity of modern life.

EXAMPLES: In the Theater of the Absurd, Eugene Ionesco's *The Bald Soprano* and Samuel Beckett's *Waiting for Godot*; in fiction, the novels of Thomas Pynchon, Joseph Heller, and Kurt Vonnegut, Jr.

accent Vocal prominence or emphasis given to a syllable, word, or phrase. In poetry accented syllables form metrical patterns by contrasting with unstressed syllables. Accented syllables are indicated by the symbol ´.

EXAMPLE: *"Cŏme líve wĭth mé ănd bé mў lóve."*
                    Marlowe

acrostic A poem in which the first letters of each line form a word, motto, or message.

EXAMPLE: <u>F</u>rom your bright sparkling Eyes I was un-
done;
<u>R</u>ays, you have; more transparent than the
Sun,
<u>A</u>midst its glory in the rising Day
<u>N</u>one can you equal in your bright array;
<u>C</u>onstant in your calm and unspotted mind,
<u>E</u>qual to all, but will to none Prove kind,
<u>S</u>o knowing, seldome one so Young, you'll
find.

George Washington

act A major division in a drama; minor divisions within an act are called scenes.

EXAMPLES: Early Greek and Roman plays, as well as those of Shakespeare's time, were divided into five acts; contemporary plays almost always have two acts.

adage A short, quotable, wise saying that is well known from wide use over a long period of time; usually of anonymous authorship.

EXAMPLES: "Haste makes waste."
"Absence makes the heart grow fonder."

See APHORISM, EPIGRAM, MAXIM, PROVERB

adaptation A literary or dramatic work rewritten for another medium.

EXAMPLES: A novel may be adapted for the stage, for motion pictures, or for television. In some cases a work originally written as a screenplay is so popular that a novel is "adapted" from the script.

affective fallacy An error that occurs when a literary critic judges a work by the degree to which it affects the emotions of the reader.

EXAMPLES: Longinus's measuring the value of a work of literature by whether or not he felt transported by it; or A.E. Housman evaluating a line of poetry by whether or not it made his whiskers bristle.

Alexandrine A line of poetry with six iambic feet, used widely in the 12th and 13th centuries to eulogize Alexander the Great. Spenser used it as a longer ninth line, following eight iambic pentameter lines, to conclude each Spenserian Stanza.

EXAMPLE: Alexander Pope parodies the use of the Alexandrine in the couplet:

> *A needless Alexandrine ends the song,*
> *That, like a wounded snake, drags its slow length*
> *along.*

See HEXAMETER

allegory A narrative poem or prose work in which persons, events, and objects represent or stand for something else.

EXAMPLES: In Bunyan's novel *Pilgrim's Progress* obstacles to the pilgrim's attempt to attain a godly life are allegorized as a bog called the Slough of Despond and the town of Vanity Fair; in George Orwell's *Animal Farm*, a herd of swine stands for a totalitarian political regime.

See ANALOGY, METAPHOR, SIMILE

alliteration The repetition of sounds in a series of words in poetry or prose.

EXAMPLES: *The <u>m</u>oan of doves in i<u>mm</u>emorial el<u>m</u>s and <u>m</u>ur<u>m</u>uring of innu<u>m</u>erable bees.*

Tennyson

<u>W</u>alking in a <u>w</u>inter <u>w</u>onderland

popular song

alliterative verse A type of poetry characteristic of the Old English, or Anglo-Saxon, period in which metrical structure is based on the repeating of initial letters or sounds within the lines.

EXAMPLE: *<u>F</u>rom a <u>f</u>riendless <u>f</u>oundling, <u>f</u>eeble and wretched,*
He grew <u>t</u>o a <u>t</u>error as <u>t</u>ime brought change.

Verse translation of Beowulf

allusion An indirect or casual reference to a famous person or event in history, the Bible, a literary work, or mythology.

EXAMPLE: An allusion is often incorporated, as in this example, in a figure of speech such as a simile or metaphor.

But sweeter than the Lids of Juno's eyes
Or Cytherea's breath.

Shakespeare

ambiguity The stating of an idea in such a way that several interpretations are possible. This is a flaw in ordinary discourse but advantageous in certain forms of literature, where meaning functions on multiple levels.

EXAMPLES: The following is a careless sentence construction leading to ambiguity: "George told Frank that he was wrong." (Who was wrong?)

The artistic use of ambiguity can be seen in this line from Gerard Manley Hopkins's poem, "God's Grandeur": "The world is charged with the grandeur of God." The multiple meanings of the word *charged* enrich the line.

anachronism The representing in literature of a person, scene, object, etc., in a time period that would have been impossible historically.

EXAMPLE: This flaw occurs even in the works of Shakespeare, who has cannons in his play *King John*, set in a period before cannons were used in England.

anacrusis The adding of an extra unstressed syllable to the beginning of a line of poetry.

EXAMPLE: The following line, made up of four trochaic feet, begins with an extra unstressed syllable, or anacrusis:

$$\breve{O}f \mid \acute{a}ll \ th\breve{e} \mid st\acute{u}pid \mid tr\acute{a}its \ of \mid teach\breve{e}rs\ldots$$

analogue Something that is like, or analogous, to another thing.

EXAMPLES: In linguistic study the word can mean a cognate, or relative of: The English word *father* is an analogue to the Latin word *pater*. In literature the *Bear's Son Tale* is an analogue to *Beowulf*, and Shakespeare's *Antony and Cleopatra* is an analogue to Dryden's *All for Love*.

analogy The comparison of one object, condition, process, or event to another in order to clarify or intensify the image or thought.

EXAMPLES: *Sleep* is frequently used as an analogy to *death*; the flowing of a river, to the passing of time; the government, to a "ship of state."

See ALLEGORY, METAPHOR, SIMILE

analytical criticism   A type of literary criticism that regards a work of art as complete and whole within itself, independent of other works of art, and even of an historical context.

See NEW CRITICISM

anapest   In poetry, a metrical foot with two unaccented syllables followed by a stressed syllable.

EXAMPLE: *"On a bénch | in the párk | in the sún | in the spríng."*

anecdote   Usually a brief account of a humorous or interesting incident.

EXAMPLES: Mark Twain's "Baker's Blue-jay Yarn" and "The Celebrated Jumping Frog of Calaveras County" are anecdotes elevated to literature.

antagonist   The rival or opponent of the hero in a work of fiction or drama.

EXAMPLE: In Shakespeare's play, Othello is the hero, or protagonist, and Iago is the antagonist.

anticlimax   The arrangement of details so that less important and trivial matters come after the most important item (rather than the usual arrangement of building up to the most important point, or climax).

EXAMPLE: Used unintentionally, anticlimax can be a serious fault in the plot of a story, but it was often used effectively for humor in satirical poetry of the 18th century, as follows:

> *Not Louder shrieks to pitying heaven are cast,*
> *When husbands, or when lap dogs breathe their*
> *last.*
>
> *Pope*

See CLIMAX

antistrophe The second part of the classical Greek choral ode; one of the stanzaic forms accompanying the strophe and the epode.

EXAMPLE: In chanting choral odes, which were an essential part of Greek drama, the chorus, with musical accompaniment, moves from right to left during the antistrophe, and in the opposite direction during the strophe. The chorus stands in place during the epode.

See EPODE, STROPHE

antithesis A rhetorical device in which sharply contrasting ideas are linked in parallel words, phrases, or clauses.

EXAMPLES: *Be not the first by whom the new are*
> *tried,*
> *Nor yet the last to lay the old aside.*
>
> *The learn'd is happy nature to explore,*
> *The fool is happy that he knows no more.*
>
> *Pope*

aphorism A statement in concise, memorable words of a principle or precept; of specific authorship.

EXAMPLES:

>   Force without mind falls by its own weight.
>
> *Horace*

>   Politics are not an exact science.
>
> *Bismarck*

See ADAGE, APOTHEGM, EPIGRAM, MAXIM, PROVERB

apostrophe In literature, the addressing of an absent person, an abstract quality (like melancholy), or a non-existent or mythological personage (like the muse) as though present.

EXAMPLE: *O Goddess! hear these tuneless numbers, wrung*
> *By sweet enforcement and remembrance dear.*
>
> *Keats*

apothegm A concisely worded and often witty saying that is instructive and usually more practical than an aphorism.

EXAMPLE:

>   Civility costs nothing and buys everything.
>
> *Lady Mary Wortly Montagu*

See ADAGE, EPIGRAM, MAXIM, PROVERB

archaisms Words, phrases, or expressions that are no longer used because they are out of date.

EXAMPLES: *Forsooth, belike,* and *parlous.*

archetypal criticism A study of a work of literature in terms of the image patterns it has in common with other works of literature, particularly those patterns which, as Northrop Frye states, recur "often enough in literature to be recognizable as an element of one's literary experience as a whole."

EXAMPLE: Jessie L. Weston's study of the Grail quest archetype, *From Ritual to Romance*.

See ARCHETYPE

argument A paragraph in prose, placed at the beginning of a long poetic work, summarizing the action which is to follow.

EXAMPLE: Milton, in his *Paradise Lost*, uses an argument at the beginning of each major subdivision of the poem. The first begins:

> This first book proposes, first in brief, the whole Subject, Man's disobedience, and the loss thereupon of Paradise wherein he was plac't: Then touches the prime cause of his fall, the Serpent, or rather Satan in the Serpent: who revolting from God, and drawing to his side many Legions of Angels, was by the command of God driven out of Heaven with all his Crew into the great Deep.

assonance A partial rhyme in which the vowel sounds are the same, but the consonant sounds are different.

EXAMPLES: *Wait, brave*; *shop, lot*; *maw, call*. In a true rhyme the vowel and end consonant sounds are the same: *wave, brave*; *shot, lot*; *mall, call*.

See CONSONANCE

autobiography A story of a person's life written by that person; also called memoirs.

EXAMPLES: The well-known autobiographies of Benjamin Franklin, Benvenuto Cellini, Henry Adams, and St. Augustine.

See BILDUNGSROMAN

ballad A poem that tells a story, often of folk origin, and is written to be sung. A ballad has simple stanzas and often a refrain.

EXAMPLES: The early American folk ballads "Barbara Allen" and "Tom Dooley." Literary ballads include Keats's "La Belle Dame Sans Merci" and Coleridge's "The Rime of the Ancient Mariner."

See REFRAIN

ballad stanza A four-line stanzaic form used in the popular ballad, or folk ballad, rhyming *abcb*. The first and third lines have accented syllables, the second and fourth only three.

EXAMPLE: *Now Robin Hood is to Nottingham gone,*
With a link-a-down and a day,
And there he met a silly old woman,
Was weeping on the way.

See REFRAIN

baroque A style in art, architecture, literature, and music characterized by flamboyancy, elaborate ornamentation, and a symmetrical arrangement. The baroque is a blend of the wild and fantastic with an ordered, formal style.

EXAMPLES: The poetry of John Donne and Richard Crashaw and the music of Bach.

beast fable A brief story in poetry or prose in which the chief characters are animals. The stories often contain moral teachings.

EXAMPLES: More recent collections of beast fables include Joel Chandler Harris's Uncle Remus stories and Rudyard Kipling's *Jungle Book* and *Just So Stories*.

See FABLE

bildungsroman A novel, usually autobiographical, that covers the principal subject's life from adolescence to maturity; also called an apprenticeship novel.

EXAMPLES: Goethe's *The Apprenticeship of Wilhelm Meister*, Dickens's *Great Expectations*, and Samuel Butler's *The Way of All Flesh*.

See AUTOBIOGRAPHY

blank verse A type of poetry in which rhyme is not used. Instead, each line has ten syllables with an iambic rhythm (an unstressed syllable followed by a stressed syllable in each poetic foot, as in "about the town").

EXAMPLES: Shakespeare's *Othello* was written in blank verse, as in this excerpt:

> *If I quench thee, thou flaming minister,*
> *I can again thy former light restore.*

Wordsworth's *The Prelude* includes the lines:

> *The leafless trees and every icy crag*
> *Tinkled like iron; while far-distant hills*
> *Into the tumult sent an alien sound*
> *Of melancholy.*

bombast Inflated, extravagant, pompous, and grandiloquent speech, found in most Elizabethan poems and plays and in many political speeches.

EXAMPLE: *O thou art fairer than the evening air,*
Clad in the beauty of a thousand stars,
Brighter art thou than flaming Jupiter,
When he appeared to hapless Semele,
More lovely than the monarch of the sky
In wanton Arethusa's azured arms,
And none but thou shalt be my paramour.

Marlowe

burlesque A form of comic drama or fiction in which an elevated subject is treated in a trivial way or a low subject is treated with mock dignity. In both cases exaggeration and distortion are used for the sake of ridicule.

EXAMPLES: Cervantes's *Don Quixote* and Beaumont and Fletcher's *The Knight of the Burning Pestle* are burlesques of medieval romances.

See COMEDY

cacophony A term used in the criticism of poetry to characterize a jarring, discordant, unharmonious combination of sounds; the opposite of euphony.

EXAMPLES: *Shrieking and squeaking*
In fifty different sharps and flats.

Browning

But when loud surges lash the sounding shore,
The hoarse, rough verse should like the torrent roar.

Pope

See EUPHONY

caesura A pause in a line of verse, usually occurring near the middle of the line. Books about the scansion of poetry traditionally indicate a caesura with a parallel slash.

EXAMPLE: *The mind is its own place, || and in itself*
Can make a Heaven of Hell, || a Hell of
Heaven.

Milton

canto A major division of a long poem; from the Latin word *cantus*, meaning song.

EXAMPLES: Spenser's *Faerie Queene* and Byron's *Childe Harold's Pilgrimage* are divided into cantos.

caricature The creation of a ridiculous effect by exaggerating particular traits of the person being satirized. Caricatures are more often found in cartoon drawings than in writing, but some characters in fiction who are not fully delineated are more caricatures than characters.

EXAMPLES: Mrs. Malaprop in Sheridan's comedy drama and Tom Jones in the Fielding novel of that name.

carpe diem A Latin phrase, meaning literally "seize the day," first used by Horace and applied to lyric poems that have the theme "Eat, drink, and be merry, for tomorrow we shall die." This was a common theme in 16th and 17th century love poetry.

EXAMPLES: Andrew Marvell's "To His Coy Mistress":
But at my back I always hear
Time's wingéd chariot hurrying near:
and
Now let us sport us while we may;

catastrophe The concluding part of a tragedy, usually involving the death of the hero. Hence, the term has come to mean a tragic event in real life.

EXAMPLES: Sophocles's *Oedipus Rex* and *Antigone* and Shakespeare's *Hamlet* all conclude with catastrophic events.

catharsis (also spelled **katharsis**) A term first used by Aristotle to describe the purging or cleansing of the emotions that a spectator experiences while attending a tragic drama. There are two interpretations of this catharsis, one being that the spectator cleanses his emotions by vicariously sharing the tragic consequences of the evil action depicted onstage and learning to avoid such action; the other holds that the spectator forgets his own conflicts and inner agitation by expending pity and fear on the tragic hero.

EXAMPLES: Spectators may feel catharsis by observing the downfall of such tragic heroes as Sophocles's Oedipus or Shakespeare's Othello. Although some literary critics would argue that Willy Loman, in Arthur Miller's *Death of a Salesman*, is not a tragic hero (because he is a traveling salesman and not a king or military leader), many theatre-goers seem to have experienced true catharsis in seeing Willy's downfall.

The Greeks also made use of the principle of catharsis outside of literature. Novice soldiers were deprived of sleep for long periods, then forced to sit while others, wearing frightening masks, screamed and danced over them. The purpose was to purge them of fear through catharsis, enabling them to go into battle unafraid.

characterization The creation of a fictional character through various techniques, including a description of his or her physical presence and actions, as well as a transcription of the character's thoughts and conversations.

EXAMPLES: E. M. Forster distinguished between flat characters, who are not fully developed and are little more than names, and round characters, who have depth and complexity. If we apply these criteria to Shakespeare's *Macbeth*, King Duncan, the victim, is a flat character, and Macbeth, the murderer, is a round character. In Dickens's novel *Oliver Twist*, Oliver is a well-rounded, fully developed character, while the Artful Dodger is a flat character, more nearly a caricature.

chorus A group of singers and dancers who appear in classical Greek and Roman dramas to provide background information and exposition of action taking place offstage; also the songs or odes sung by the chorus.

EXAMPLES: Any drama by Aeschylus, Sophocles, or Euripides provides abundant examples of choruses. From Elizabethan times onward, the role of the chorus was taken over by a single actor, when comments on the action were necessary to the dramatist's purpose. Recent examples include Thornton Wilder's *Our Town* and T. S. Eliot's *Murder in the Cathedral*. In Marlowe's *Doctor Faustus*, an introductory prologue is spoken by one actor, but the prologue, in the text of the play, is called a "chorus."

classical tragedy A tragic play written in ancient Greece or Rome, or a modern tragedy based on Greek or Roman subjects of the classical age.

EXAMPLES: An example of the former is Sophocles's *Antigone*; of the latter, Shakespeare's *Coriolanus*.

classicism The philosophy of art associated with the ancient Greeks and Romans, typically characterized by the following qualities: balance, moderation, self-control, dominance of reason, unity of design and purpose, clarity, simplicity, and respect for tradition.

EXAMPLES: The masters of classicism are Virgil and Homer, followed by Ben Jonson, the chief advocate of classicism in the Renaissance, and by John Dryden, Alexander Pope, and Samuel Johnson in the Restoration and Augustan Ages.

climax The point of highest interest or conflict in the plot of a short story, novel, or play. A climactic arrangement of words and phrases in a sentence has the ideas occurring in an order of rising importance, with the most important item being the climax.

EXAMPLES: "In the battle there were 46 wounded, 24 missing in action, and 31 killed." In a murder mystery the climax occurs just before the mystery is explained.

closed couplet A pair of rhymed lines of poetry containing a complete statement, structurally independent of lines that come before and after.

EXAMPLES: *Had we but world enough, and time,*
This coyness, lady, were no crime.
                                                        Marvell
Be thou the first true merit to defend,
His praise is lost, who stays till all
    commend.
                                                        Pope

All human things are subject to decay,
And when fate summons, monarchs
must obey.

Dryden

closet drama A dramatic work, usually written in poetry, intended to be read rather than acted on the stage.

EXAMPLES: Browning's *Pippa Passes*, Shelley's *The Cenci*, Milton's *Samson Agonistes*. Contemporary writers of plays write only for performance before an audience, and the closet drama is virtually obsolete.

comedy A branch of drama or fiction in which the characters are treated humorously. There is a happy ending, and the audience is amused.

EXAMPLES: Works as varied as Shakespeare's *Two Gentlemen of Verona*, Shaw's *Pygmalion* (the basis of the musical comedy *My Fair Lady*), and Neil Simon's *The Odd Couple*. It should be noted that Shaw's comedies were intended to produce "thoughtful laughter." Beneath the frivolity was a serious purpose.

See BURLESQUE, COMEDY OF MANNERS, COMEDY OF SITUATION, FARCE

comedy of manners A type of satirical comedy, especially popular in the Restoration and neoclassical periods, concerned with the manners of a highly sophisticated and artificial society and characterized by witty dialogue.

EXAMPLES: Congreve's *The Way of the World* and Sheridan's *The Rivals* and *The School for Scandal* are typical comedies of manners, as is Oscar Wilde's more recent *The Importance of Being Earnest*. In a real sense, "M.A.S.H," the long-running comedy series on television, was like a comedy of manners in that it dealt with the structured society of the army in wartime and much of its sophisticated humor was based on the artificial, unreal nature of that society.

comedy of situation   Usually a comedy in which the plot or the situation in which the characters are placed is more important than characterization. Although modern television "sitcoms" (situation comedies) have a continuing set of more or less well-defined characters, they typify this kind of comedy.

EXAMPLE: Shakespeare's *The Comedy of Errors* exploits the situation of mistaken identities arising when two identical twins have servants who are identical twins. A comic situation that has been used in several movies portrays a character who makes a bet that he will speak only the absolute truth for the period of 24 hours. One can imagine the comic scenes deriving from this premise.

comic relief   A comic scene or incident that a playwright inserts in a serious drama to relieve tension and to provide a contrast to the seriousness of the play.

EXAMPLES: The gravedigger scene in *Hamlet*, the speeches of Mercutio in *Romeo and Juliet*, and the scene with the drunken porter in *Macbeth*.

complication   In drama, the development of the conflict of opposing forces—also called rising action—leading to a climax and a resolution.

EXAMPLE: If the conflict in a story is, for example, a

mountain climber against a mountain, the complication builds when the climber slips, a rope breaks, and he is trapped on a narrow ledge. Many conventional romantic stories are briefly summarized as "Boy meets girl, boy loses girl, boy marries girl." The middle of the sequence, "boy loses girl," is the complication.

conflict In drama or fiction, the collision between opposing forces (usually the protagonist against the antagonist).

EXAMPLES: The hero against the villain, a human being against nature, a person against a community. In Henrik Ibsen's play *An Enemy of the People*, Dr. Stockmann discovers that the water in the town is contaminated by the local sewage system. When he tries to reveal the truth, he is in conflict with the town authorities, who believe the truth will harm the tourist business. A classic conflict in early English literature has the hero Beowulf fighting to the death with a monster named Grendel.

consonance In poetry, the agreement of the final consonant sounds when the vowel sounds are different.

EXAMPLES: *Mile, till; cow, low; moat, late*. To form a true rhyme, the vowel and final consonant sounds must be the same: *mill, till; flow, low; mate, late*.

See ASSONANCE

controlling image A metaphor or other figure of speech which is found throughout a literary work and gives it form and focus.

EXAMPLE: *"On a Girdle"*

That which her slender waist confined,
Shall now my joyful temples bind;
No monarch but would give his crown,
His arms might do what this has done.

   It was my heaven's extremest sphere,
The pale which held that lovely deer;
My joy, my grief, my hope, my love
Did all within this circle move!

   A narrow compass! and yet here
Dwelt all that's good, and all that's fair;
Give me but what this ribbon bound,
Take all the rest the sun goes round!
                                                   Edmund Waller

See METAPHOR

convention A literary practice, style, or technique that has become, through frequent use, an accepted method of literary expression.

EXAMPLES: In drama, the soliloquy, in which a character speaks to the audience but is accepted as being unheard by the other characters on stage; the "fourth wall" (the proscenium arch) of the stage through which the audience watches the action. Fainting heroines and happy endings at which a number of characters are joined in marriage are conventions of Victorian fiction. In the novels of Charles Dickens, for example, there are often mass wedding ceremonies in the final pages in which not only the main characters are paired off, but the servants and minor characters as well.

couplet Two rhyming lines of poetry, usually in lines of eight or ten syllables each.

EXAMPLES: The following stanza from Ben Jonson's

"Still to Be Neat" is written in octosyllabic couplets:

> *Give me a look, give me a face*
> *That makes simplicity a grace;*
> *Robes loosely flowing, hair as free;*
> *Such sweet neglect more taketh me*
> *Than all the adulteries of art.*
> *They strike mine eyes, but not my heart.*

The iambic pentameter couplet (with ten syllables) was the predominant poetic form of Eighteenth Century English literature, as typified by the following couplets of Pope:

> *Heaven from all creatures hides the book of fate,*
> *All but the page prescribed, their present state:*
> *From brutes what men, from men what spirits*
> *   know:*
> *Or who could suffer being here below?*
> *The lamb thy riot dooms to bleed today,*
> *Had he thy reason, would he skip and play?*
> *Pleased to the last, he crops the flowery food*
> *And licks the hand just raised to shed his blood.*

crisis In the plot of a novel or play, the point at which the hero must either win or lose; the decisive moment of the conflict.

EXAMPLE: In a western drama the conflict between the hero and villain builds to a crisis scene in which the two shoot it out: the fastest draw wins.

cycle A term—which originally meant "circle"— used to describe a collection of poems or romances surrounding an outstanding character or event.

EXAMPLES: The "Cycle of Lancelot" and the epics about Charlemagne.

dactyl A foot in poetry that has one accented syllable followed by two unaccented ones.

EXAMPLES: *Cárrў̆ĭng, béără̆blĕ.*

decadence A term used by literary historians to denote the decline that signals the end of a great period in literature, characterized by such qualities as abnormal and artificial subject matter, extreme self-consciousness, and an overly subtilized style.

EXAMPLES: The French writers Verlaine, Rimbaud, and Baudelaire and the English writers Wilde, Dowson, and Beardsley are among the decadent writers of the late 19th and early 20th centuries.

decorum A critical term used to describe what is fitting and proper for a character, subject, or setting in a literary work.

EXAMPLES: The angels in Milton's *Paradise Lost* and the kings in Greek and Shakespearean tragedies speak in an appropriate, highly rhetorical style, not in the colloquial manner suitable for characters like Huck Finn or Samuel Weller.

denouement Literally, the "untying of the knot"; the final outcome, solution, or unraveling of the principal dramatic conflict in a literary work.

EXAMPLES: Typical denouements are the solution of a problem or mystery, the reunion of separated persons, and the correction of mistaken identities. *The Moonstone*, by Wilkie Collins, acclaimed by T. S. Eliot as "the first, the longest, and the best of modern English detective novels," has a long denouement in which the sleuth, Sergeant Cuff of Scotland Yard, deduces that an enormous diamond had been stolen by a man who was under sedation and had no way of stealing the stone and passing it to the real culprit.

deus ex machina Literally, "god from a machine"; the use of an unexpected and unforeshadowed person or thing to provide a contrived, artificial solution to a dramatic conflict that is often apparently unsolvable.

EXAMPLE: In early Greek drama, when the conflict became hopeless, a god was lowered to the stage from a "machine" or structure above to rescue the hero and take him up and out of the problem.

In more recent literature the use of the *deus ex machina* indicates that the author is inadequate in his devising of a plot. In late Victorian melodramas, when a long-lost relative, newly wealthy, appears on the scene just in time to save the family farm from being sold by the sheriff, the *deus ex machina* is exemplified.

dialogue Conversation between two or more characters, common in fiction and drama; also used in philosophical writing.

EXAMPLES: Conventional novels, short stories, dramas, and movies. Plato's *Dialogues*, Lucian's *Dialogues of the Dead* and Landor's *Imaginary Conversations* exemplify the second meaning.

See MONOLOGUE

didactic A term used to describe poetic works whose primary objective is to teach or to convey moral observations.

EXAMPLES: Pope's *Essay on Criticism*, Gray's "Elegy Written in a Country Churchyard."

dirge A brief song or lyric of lamentation, usually intended to accompany funeral rites.

EXAMPLES: Tennyson's "Tears, Idle Tears"; in music, Chopin's "Funeral March."

dissonance A harsh, unpleasant sound used in poetry, sometimes intentionally for effect, as in the poetry of Browning.

EXAMPLE: *Fee, faw, fum! bubble and squeak!*
              Blessedest Thursday's the fat of the week.
              Rumble and tumble, sleek and rough,
              Stinking and savory, smug and gruff.
                                              Browning

See CACOPHONY

dramatic irony In drama, the irony perceived by an audience when a character makes statements not fully understood by himself.

EXAMPLE: A character might remark on the uncertainty of life, not knowing (as the audience does) that a maniacal killer is at that moment stalking him. In Shakespeare's *Othello*, Act III, scene iii, the audience knows that Iago is about to deceive the hero in a terrible way, but Othello says of Iago: "I know thou'rt full of love and honesty." This adds to the dramatic tension, and the audience enjoys its special knowledge and perception of the scene.

dramatic monologue A type of lyrical poem that has a person speaking to a silent listener and revealing his character in a dramatic situation.

EXAMPLES: Most of the poems of Browning (who brought the dramatic monologue to its highest level), and T. S. Eliot's "Love Song of J. Alfred Prufrock." Two of Browning's best-known examples are the monologues of famous Italian Renaissance painters: "Andrea del Sarto" and "Fra Lippo Lippi."

eclogue A type of formal pastoral poem characterized by two shepherds having a singing match to settle a wager, or a rustic dialogue between two shepherds concerning their mistresses or their flocks, or a dirge or lament for a dead shepherd.

EXAMPLES: Virgil's pastoral poems; the best-known examples in English comprise Spenser's *The Shepheardes Calender*, which has an eclogue for each month of the year. In the August eclogue, two shepherds converse:

WILLYE

Tell me Perigot, what shalbe the game,
Wherefore with myne thou dare thy musick
matche?
Or bene thy Bagpypes renne farre out of frame?
Or has the Crampe thy joynts benomd with ache?

PERIGOT

Ah Willye, when the hart is ill assayde,
How can Bagpype or joints be well apayd?

elegy A long and formal poem meditating on the dead; often written to commemorate the death of a particular person.

EXAMPLES: Gray's "Elegy in a Country Churchyard" mourns the unknown dead buried in a quiet churchyard; Tennyson's *In Memoriam* and Whitman's "When

Lilacs Last in the Dooryard Bloom'd" are elegies about
the deaths of specific persons, Arthur Henry Hallam
and President Lincoln.

elision The omission of a part of a word to make pronunciation easier or to achieve a rhythmic effect.

EXAMPLES: *e'er* for *ever*, *there's* for *there is*.

empathy The sharing of physical and emotional feel-
ings by identifying with a character in literature or a
person in real life.

EXAMPLE: If one feels the hunger and misery of the
principal characters in Dickens's *Oliver Twist* or *David
Copperfield*, one experiences empathy.

end-rhyme Rhymes occurring at the ends of lines of
poetry, which is the usual case.

EXAMPLE: *I was angry with my friend:*
          I told my wrath, my wrath did end.
          I was angry with my foe:
          I told it not, my wrath did grow.
                                            Blake

end-stopped line A line of poetry in which the idea
is complete and which ends with a punctuation mark.

EXAMPLES: *Delusive Fortune hears the incessant call,*
          They mount, they shine, evaporate and fall.
                                    Samuel Johnson
          My former thoughts returned: the fear that
             kills;
          And hope that is unwilling to be fed;
                                    William Wordsworth

epic An extended narrative poem, written in an elevated style, recounting the deeds of a legendary or actual hero.

EXAMPLES: Homer's the *Iliad* and the *Odyssey*, Vergil's *Aeneid*, and Milton's *Paradise Lost*.

See MOCK EPIC

epic simile A comparison that differs from an ordinary simile in that it is much lengthier, more complex, and consciously imitative of the kind of similes used by Homer in his epic poems.

EXAMPLES: *As, in the country, on a morn in June,*
             When the dew glistens on the pearled ears,
             A shiver runs through the deep corn for
                 joy—
             So, when they heard what Peran-Wisa said,
             A thrill through all the Tartar squadrons ran
             Of pride and hope for Sohrab, whom they
                 loved.

                                        Matthew Arnold

             Thus they their doubtful consultations dark
             Ended rejoicing in their matchless chief:
             As when from mountain tops the dusky
                 clouds
             Ascending while the North wind sleeps, o'er-
                 spread
             Heaven's cheerful face, the low'ring Element
             Scowls o'er the dark'n'd landskip snow, or
                 show'r;
             If chance the radiant Sun with farewell sweet
             Extend his ev'ning beam, the fields revive,

> *The birds their notes renew, and bleating*
> *herds*
> *Attest their joy, that hill and valley rings.*
>   *John Milton*

See SIMILE

epigram A short poem, often satirical, dealing with a single thought or event and ending with a clever turn of phrase; also, a short, witty, and often paradoxical saying.

EXAMPLES: Ben Jonson, whose model was the Roman poet Martial, is the most famous English writer of poetic epigrams, as demonstrated by the lines below:

> *He that for love of goodness hateth ill*
> *Is more crown-worthy still*
> *Than he which for sin's penalty forbears;*
> *His heart sins, though he fears.*

The following is an epigrammatic saying:

> The greatest pleasure I know is to do a good action by stealth and to have it found out by accident.
>
>   *Charles Lamb*

See ADAGE, APHORISM, PROVERB

epilogue A concluding section that completes the design of a literary work; also a speech in early drama spoken by an actor addressing the audience at the conclusion of a play.

EXAMPLE: At the end of Shakespeare's *A Midsummer Night's Dream*, Puck addresses the audience in an epilogue that begins:

> *If we shadows have offended,*
> *Think but this, and all is mended,*

That you have but slumbered here,
While there visions did appear.

epistolary novel A novel in which the story is carried forward entirely through letters from one or more persons.

EXAMPLES: Several of the earliest English novels were epistolary, including Samuel Richardson's *Pamela* (1740) and *Clarissa Harlowe* (1748).

epithalamium (or **epithalamion**) A song or poem written to honor a bride and bridegroom.

EXAMPLE: Spenser's *Epithalamion*, written to celebrate his own wedding, is considered to be the finest of the English marriage hymns. The following is an excerpt:
   Now is my love all ready forth to come,
   Let all the virgins therefore well awayt,
   And ye fresh boyes that tend upon her groome
   Prepare your selves; for he is coming strayt.
   Set all your things in seemely good aray
   Fit for so joyfull day,
   The joyfulst day that ever sunne did see.

epode The third part of the classical Greek choral ode, coming after the strophe and antistrophe; the chorus stands in place when reciting the epode section.

EXAMPLE: Pindar's odes celebrating the Olympiads of Greece contain strophes, antistrophes, and epodes.

See ANTISTROPHE, STROPHE

eponym A person, real or mythical, who is so commonly associated with a certain characteristic that his or her name becomes a figure of speech for that attribute.

EXAMPLES: "He is an Adonis" means that a man is handsome; "She is a Helen" means that a woman is beautiful.

essay A prose composition, usually brief, dealing with a particular theme or topic. Essays vary widely and may be descriptive, narrative, expository, or argumentative.

EXAMPLES: The informal essay, often called the "true essay," is well represented in English literature and includes Steele's "A Cure for Fits in Married Ladies," Lamb's "A Dissertation on Roast Pig," and Hazlitt's "On Going on a Journey."

See FORMAL ESSAY, INFORMAL ESSAY, PERSONAL ESSAY

euphemism The substitution of an innocuous or pleasant word or phrase for one considered offensive or impolite.

EXAMPLES: *passed away* for *died*; *in a family way* for *pregnant.*

euphony A pleasing and harmonious combination of sounds. Euphonious phrases avoid excessive alliteration and the stringing together of harsh consonants and unaccented syllables, and use instead combinations that are felicitous to the ear.

EXAMPLE: *Come and trip it as you go*
On the light fantastic toe.
　　　　　　　　　　Milton
Whenas in silks my Julia goes,
Then, then methinks how sweetly flows
The liquefaction of her clothes.

See CACOPHONY
　　　　　　　　　　　　　　Herrick

euphuism An artificial, affected literary style, popular in the late 16th century in England, characterized by excessive alliteration, balanced constructions, and rhetorical questions.

EXAMPLES: From John Lyly's *Euphues: The Anatomy of Wit*:

> I have found such flames that I can neither quench them with the water of free will, neither cool them with wisdom.

• • •

> But as the true gold is tried by the touch, the pure flint by the stroke of the iron, so the loyal heart of the faithful lover is known by the trial of his lady.

existentialism A philosophical position, espoused by Kierkegaard, Heidegger, and Sartre, that presupposes one has free will and is therefore completely responsible for one's actions. Existentialists believe that one forms one's essential being (or essence) by choosing a particular course and pattern in life.

EXAMPLES: Sartre's plays *The Flies* and *No Exit* broach the problem of human freedom and responsibility; Camus's story *The Fall* explores the problem of man's guilt and the extent of his freedom.

explication de texte A method of teaching and evaluating literature that originated in France and which consists of a careful analysis of the meaning of words and images in a work. A favorite tool of the New Critics, this method is the primary thrust of the important book *Understanding Poetry* by Cleanth Brooks and Robert Penn Warren.

See NEW CRITICS

expressionism A literary movement of the early 20th century, found mostly in drama, dedicated to revealing the depths of the human mind (after the discoveries of depth psychologists like Freud). Expressionist theater uses unreal atmospheres, distortion, and oversimplification to depict external representations of extreme psychological states.

EXAMPLES: Strindberg's *The Dream Play*, O'Neill's *The Hairy Ape*, Rice's *The Adding Machine*.

eye-rhyme Words that appear from the spellings to rhyme, but are actually half-rhymes or slant-rhymes because they are not pronounced as rhymes.

EXAMPLES: *love*, *prove*; *latch*, *watch*.

fable A brief tale in prose or poetry that emphasizes a moral and usually has animals as the principal characters.

EXAMPLES: Aesop's *Fables*, Joel Chandler Harris's Uncle Remus stories. In one such tale, Remus has a bear entrap a rabbit when his curiosity causes him to be stuck in an effigy of a baby made of tar. The rabbit makes his escape by pleading with the bear not to throw him in the briar patch, which the bear cannot resist doing. The briar patch being the rabbit's natural habitat, the rabbit laughs and taunts the bear as he runs away. The moral is that brains can be more important than brute strength.

fabliau A short comic tale in verse, often coarse in content, popular in French literature of the 12th and 13th centuries.

EXAMPLES: Chaucer's *Canterbury Tales* provides a rich

collection of *fabliaux* in the tales of the Miller, Reeve, Friar, and Summoner.

falling action The point in the plot of a story or drama that comes after the climax; also called the resolution.

EXAMPLE: A story involving the hero and villain in a life-and-death struggle reaches a climax when one of them wins. What happens after this is a falling action, or resolution.

fantasy Any literature in a non-existent or unreal world, which has characters that are incredible and unreal or employs fanciful scientific principles.

EXAMPLES: Fairy tales by the Grimm Brothers, Barrie's *Peter Pan*, and most science fiction stories.
   The movies *Star Wars* and *Return of the Jedi* are fantasies.

farce A type of low comedy with broad and obvious satire and humor and much physical action.

EXAMPLE: One of the most famous farces is Brandon Thomas's *Charley's Aunt* (1892), which deals with comical events resulting from a female impersonation.

See BURLESQUE

feminine ending An unstressed syllable added to the end of a line of poetry in iambic or anapestic meter (which would ordinarily end with a stressed syllable) for variety's sake.

EXAMPLE: The second couplet of the following verse:
   He spoke of the grass and flowers and trees,

Of the singing birds and the humming bees;
Then talked of the haying, and wondered whether
The cloud in the west would bring foul weather.
                                                    Author unknown

feminine rhyme Any two rhyming words containing one stressed and one or more unstressed syllables.

EXAMPLES: *breaking*, *waking*; *posing*, *closing*; *intuition*, *remission*.

figurative language Language that is not meant to be taken literally; used by an author to clarify and intensify an image.

EXAMPLES: "He is a *tiger* when he is angry" and "He eats *like a horse*" have become commonplace in conversation.
    Literary examples include
        The soul's dark cottage, batter'd and decay'd
        Lets in new light through chinks that time has
            made.
                                                    Edmund Waller
        A white bird, she told him once, looking at him
        gravely, a bird he must carry in his bosom
        across a crowded public place—his own soul
        was like that!
                                                    Walter Pater

flashback An interruption of the narrative flow in order to present scenes or incidents that occurred prior to the beginning of the novel or short story.

EXAMPLE: Hemingway's short story "The Snows of Kilimanjaro" begins with the hero severely injured and lying on a cot, his mind dreamily dredging up scenes from the past in flashbacks.

Many dramas, such as Arthur Miller's *The American Clock*, portray past actions by showing them onstage in flashbacks.

foot A unit of rhythm in poetry.

EXAMPLES: Usually a foot has one stressed syllable and one or more unstressed syllables: *away* (iambic), *flaming* (trochaic), *in the ditch* (anapestic), and *merrily* (dactylic).

formal essay An essay written in an elevated, formal style on a serious subject.

EXAMPLES: Milton's *Areopagitica*, Locke's *Essay on the Human Understanding*.

See INFORMAL ESSAY

free verse Poetic compositions in which there is neither rhyme nor a regular meter; also called *vers libre* (Latin for free verse).

EXAMPLES: Most of the poems of Walt Whitman and Carl Sandburg.

genre A term used by literary critics to indicate the various categories in which literary works are grouped by form; from the French word for kind or type.

EXAMPLES: Literary genres include the epic, the lyric, tragedy, comedy, and the picaresque novel.

ghost-writer One who writes a book or article that is published under the name of another, usually more well-known, person. Most of the so-called autobiographies of movie stars and sports figures are ghost-written.

gloss An explanation in the margin or between the lines of difficult works to explain obscure meanings by substituting a familiar word or phrase for an obscure one.

EXAMPLE: The famous marginal gloss of Coleridge's *The Rime of the Ancient Mariner* begins, "An ancient Mariner meeteth three Gallants bidden to a wedding feast, and detaineth one."

gothic novel A type of novel, first popularized in the late 18th century, characterized by thrill-provoking and supernatural events, often taking place in a medieval castle.

EXAMPLES: Horace Walpole's *Castle of Otranto* (the first of the genre), Anne Radcliffe's *The Mysteries of Udolpho*, Mary Shelley's *Frankenstein*. A paragraph from Walpole's novel demonstrates the exaggeration and heightened emotionalism of the style:

> Shocked with these lamentable sounds, and dreading he knew not what, he advanced hastily—but, what a sight for a father's eyes!— he beheld his child dashed to pieces, and almost buried under an enormous helmet, a hundred times more large than any casque ever made for human being, and shaded with a proportionable quantity of black feathers.

grotesque A term originally applied to distorted and fantastic representations of human and animal forms in sculpture and architecture: e.g., gargoyles on medieval cathedrals. Applied to literature, the word has come to denote characters who are spiritually or physically deformed or similarly abnormal in their actions.

EXAMPLES: Browning's poem "Soliloquy in a Spanish Cloister" and Flannery O'Connor's novel *Wise Blood*.

haiku (also written **hokku**) A genre of Japanese poetry in which three lines of exactly five, seven, and five syllables, respectively, are used to present a picture that elicits an emotional response and a specific spiritual insight.

EXAMPLE: *Lightning in the sky!*
In the deeper dark is heard
A night-heron's call.
                    Basho

half-rhyme An imperfect rhyme in which there may be a similarity of consonance or assonance but not a true rhyme.

EXAMPLES: *gold*, *note* (dissonance because the vowel sounds are the same); *will*, *style* (consonance because the final consonant sounds agree).

See ASSONANCE, CONSONANCE, DISSONANCE

heptameter A line of poetry with seven feet.

EXAMPLE: *Of áll thĕ váin ŭnríghtĕous tráits*
of mán ŭnkínd ănd méan,

heroic couplet A pair of rhymed lines written in iambic pentameter.

EXAMPLES: *Alas! in truth the man but changed his*
*   mind,*
*   Perhaps was sick, in love, or had not*
*   dined.*
                    Pope

A time there was ere England's griefs began,
When every rood of ground maintain'd its
    man.
                                                                    Goldsmith
Pernicious weed! whose scent the fair
    annoys,
Unfriendly to society's chief joys,
Thy worst effect is banishing for hours
The sex whose presence civilizes ours.
                                                                    Cowper

hexameter In classical Latin and Greek poetry, an elaborately patterned, rhythmic line; now merely a line of poetry with six metrical feet. Alexandrines are hexameter lines.

EXAMPLE: The third line of the following is a hexameter.
    His looser garment to the ground did fall,
    And flew about his heels in wanton wise,
    Not fit for speedy pace, or manly exercise.
                                                                    Spenser
See ALEXANDRINE

historicism A type of literary criticism that examines the historical context in which a work was produced, and attempts to determine the influence of social and cultural forces on that work. Another form of *historicism* attempts to ascertain the applicability of a literary work of the past to present-day readers.

EXAMPLES: The literary criticism of Roy Harvey Pearce and William Morris.

Horatian ode An ode in which each stanza follows the same metrical pattern.
EXAMPLE: Keats's *Ode to a Nightingale*.

See IRREGULAR ODE, PINDARIC ODE

hubris (also spelled **hybris**) A Greek term that denotes the excessive pride leading to the downfall of the hero in a tragic drama.

EXAMPLE: Macbeth's pride and excessive ambition, which led to calamitous results. Doctor Faustus, whose pride led him to sell his soul to the devil in exchange for power and magical knowledge.

hyperbole A figure of speech characterized by deliberate exaggeration; not to be taken literally.

EXAMPLES: "I've told you a thousand times."

> All the perfumes of Arabia will not sweeten this little hand.
>
> *Shakespeare*

iambic A metrical foot that has two syllables, with the accent or stress on the second. The term is used in conjunction with another word to denote the rhythm and number of stressed syllables in a line of poetry: e.g., iambic pentameter (five iambic feet).

EXAMPLES: *agáin, promóte, enfórce.*

imagery A term used frequently in literary criticism to refer either to figures of speech or to verbal representations of sensory objects or sensations.

EXAMPLES: Both types of imagery can be found in Keats's poem "The Eve of St. Agnes":
Literal:

> The hare limped trembling through the frozen grass,
> And silent was the flock in wooly fold:

Figure of speech:

> ... his frosted breath,
> Like pious incense from a censer old,
> Seemed taking flight for heaven, without death.

imagination The mental faculty of forming images. During the Renaissance the word denoted the poetic faculty as opposed to reason and rationality; in the 18th century imagination meant only the faculty of calling up images to the mind; in the Romantic period Coleridge and Wordsworth made the term more complex by including all the powers of the mind that enable poets to see inner relationships, such as the essence of truth and beauty.

EXAMPLES: Bacon, in the the Renaissance, wrote that "history has reference to the memory, poetry to the imagination"; Joseph Addison's *The Pleasures of the Imagination* refers to the pleasures of calling up images; Coleridge called imagination the "shaping and modifying" power.

See FANCY

imagists A group of American poets prominent from 1909–1918 and dedicated to producing poems employing the language of common speech, new rhythms, new subject matter, and strong concrete imagery.

EXAMPLES: The poets Carl Sandburg, William Carlos Williams, Ezra Pound, and Amy Lowell.

imitation A concept of art that originated with Aristotle's dictum that art imitates nature. The term also refers to the practice—acceptable in the Greek and Roman schools of rhetoric—of learning composition by imitating literary models.

EXAMPLES: The imitation of nature in painting and literature leads to realistic representations of what the artist sees, not abstract compositions. Samuel Johnson imitated the form of Addison's prose essays by attempting to rewrite them in his own words, then rewriting that version to conform as closely as possible to the original.

impressionistic criticism A type of literary criticism that emphasizes the critic's feelings and emotions in the presence of a work of art.

EXAMPLES: Thomas DeQuincey's essay, "On the Knocking at the Gate in Macbeth." John Ruskin's essay on J.M.W. Turner's painting "The Slave Ship" (from *Modern Painters*). Ruskin's emotional style of criticism is demonstrated in the following excerpt:

> Great art is precisely that which never was, nor will be taught, it is preeminently and finally the expression of the spirits of great men; so that the only wholesome teaching is that which simply endeavors to fix those characters of nobleness in the pupil's mind, of which it seems easily susceptible; and without holding out to him, as a possible or even probable result, that he should ever paint like Titian, or carve like Michael Angelo, enforces upon him the manifest possibility, and assured duty, of endeavoring to draw in a manner at least honest and intelligible; and cultivates in him those general charities of heart, sincerities of thought, and graces of habit which are likely to lead him, throughout life, to prefer openness to affectation, realities to shadows, and beauty to corruption.

influence A term used by literary historians to denote the effect of a writer, or school of writers, on the work of another author or authors.

EXAMPLES: The influence of Milton's poetry on Wordsworth's works and Shakespeare's works on those of Keats.

informal essay An essay that is usually brief and has a purpose that is less serious than a formal essay's. It is written in a light and easy style.

EXAMPLES: Leigh Hunt's "On Getting Up on Cold Mornings." Charles Lamb's "A Chapter on Ears."

See FORMAL ESSAY

intentional fallacy A term associated with the New Criticism, which uses it to describe the error or fallacy that occurs when one judges a literary work according to what the author says he intended—statements by authors being subject to the same rigorous scrutiny as other testimony. Originated by M. C. Beardsley and W. K. Wimsatt, Jr., the term is elaborated upon in Wimsatt's *The Verbal Icon*.

See NEW CRITICISM

interior monologue A technique used in the writing of a novel or short story to record the inner thoughts and emotional responses of a character; also called stream of consciousness.

EXAMPLES: Virginia Woolf's novels and the Molly Bloom section of James Joyce's *Ulysses*, which is perhaps the best-known example.

See STREAM-OF-CONSCIOUSNESS NOVEL

inversion A rhetorical device in which a sentence element is placed out of its usual position for the sake of emphasis or poetic effect; also, the inverting of the order of a sentence for effect.

EXAMPLE: *At midnight on the Emperor's pavement flit*
Flames that no faggot feeds, nor steel has lit

Yeats

irony A rhetorical device in which the author conveys a meaning opposite to the words actually used.

EXAMPLES: Passenger to driver, immediately after a fender-bending accident: "What a great driver you are!" In Shakespeare's *Julius Caesar*, during his oration over the dead Caesar, Antony says, "Brutus is an honorable man," when referring to the emperor's murderer.

irregular ode A type of ode that does not adhere to the strophe, antistrophe, epode pattern of the Pindaric Ode or the stanzaic repetition of the Horatian Ode; also, stanzaic forms freely varied in number and length.

EXAMPLE: Wordsworth's "Ode on Intimations of Immortality."

See HORATIAN ODE, PINDARIC ODE

Italian sonnet Also called the Petrarchan sonnet, this type of sonnet is divided into an octave, which always rhymes *abbaabba*, and a sestet, which usually rhymes *cdecde*.

EXAMPLE:

> *"On His Blindness"*
> *When I consider how my light is spent*
> *Ere half my days in this dark world and wide,*
> *And that one talent which is death to hide*
> *Lodged with me useless, though my soul more*
> *   bent*
> *To serve therewith my Maker, and present*
> *My true account, lest He returning chide,*
> *"Doth God exact day-labor, light denied?"*
> *I fondly ask. But Patience, to prevent*
> *That murmur, soon replies, "God doth not need*
> *Either man's work or his own gifts. Who best*
> *Bear his mild yoke, they serve him best. His state*
> *Is kingly: thousands at his bidding speed,*
> *And post o'er land and ocean without rest;*
> *They also serve who only stand and wait."*
>
>   *Milton*

kenning A type of phrase found in Old English poetry as a figure of speech to stand for a simple noun. It embellishes ordinary words used to stand for objects and persons.

EXAMPLES: *the whale-road* for sea, the *storm of swords* for battle (both from *Beowulf*).

lay A short song, sometimes a historical ballad, associated with the earlier songs and verse tales sung by Breton minstrels on themes that come from ancient legends.

EXAMPLES: Scott's *Lay of the Last Minstrel* and Macaulay's *Lays of Ancient Rome*.

lexicography The editing or the making of a dictionary, or lexicon; the principles of dictionary making.

EXAMPLE: Samuel Johnson's *Dictionary of the English Language* (1755) is considered the most important early work of lexicography in English.

lexicon A book containing, in alphabetical order, the words of a language and their definitions; a dictionary.

EXAMPLE: The most ancient dictionary is said to be a Greek lexicon called *Homeric Words*, written in 27 B.C.–A.D. 14.

libretto The text, spoken and sung, of a work for the musical theater, such as an opera, an operetta, or a musical comedy.

EXAMPLES: Salvatore Cammarano wrote the libretto for Verdi's opera *Il Trovatore*; Sir William S. Gilbert wrote the libretti for Sir Arthur Sullivan's music in the Gilbert and Sullivan comic operas; Richard Rodgers wrote the music and Oscar Hammerstein the libretti and lyrics for such musical comedies as *Oklahoma!*, *The King and I*, and *South Pacific*.

light verse A type of poetry, usually short and humorous, which comes in many different varieties, including parody, epigrams, and limericks.

EXAMPLE: The clerihew, named for G. Clerihew Bentley, has four lines rhyming in couplets and gives a brief biography of a well-known person, as in the following:

Sir Isaac Newton
Had no time for rootin' and tootin'.
What did he do instead?
He let apples fall on his head.

See LIMERICK

limerick A humorous five-line poem rhyming *aabba*, with lines one, two, and five having three anapestic feet, and lines three and four, two anapestic feet. A limerick is sometimes written in four lines, combining the two short lines into one.

EXAMPLE: *There was a young lady of Tottenham,*
Who'd no manners, or else she'd forgotten
'em;
At tea at the vicar's
She tore off her knickers,
Because, she explained, she felt 'ot in 'em.

litotes A figure of speech that uses understatement to make a point stronger, usually by stating the opposite of the point being affirmed.

EXAMPLES: "Einstein was not one of your most stupid scientists," or "New York cheesecake is not a bad dessert." In the Book of the Acts of the Apostles in the Bible is found the example, "A citizen of no mean city."

lyric A short, melodic, imaginative poem, usually characterized by intense personal emotion, that creates for the reader a unified impression. Lyric poems include sonnets, songs, ballads, odes, and elegies.

EXAMPLES: Wordsworth's "I Wandered Lonely as a Cloud," Keats's "Ode on a Grecian Urn," Shelley's "To a Skylark."

madrigal A short lyric, usually designed to be sung with musical accompaniment, which generally has a pastoral or love motif. In Elizabethan times madrigals were sung a cappella by five or six voices, with a complex interweaving of words and melody. Italian madrigals are written in a pattern of from six to thirteen lines, with three rhymes.

EXAMPLES: Orlando Gibbons's "The Silver Swan," Shakespeare's "Take, O, take those lips away" from *Measure for Measure.*

malapropism A humorous misuse of language that results from substituting an incorrect word for one with a similar sound; named for a character, Mrs. Malaprop, in Richard Sheridan's comedy, *The Rivals.*

EXAMPLE: Sir Anthony Absolute says that Mrs. Malaprop tends to "deck her dull chat with hard words which she don't understand," whereat Mrs. Malaprop rejoins: "Sure, if I reprehend any thing in this world, it is the use of my oracular tongue, and a nice derangement of epitaphs!"

masculine rhyme Rhyme in which the corresponding sounds occur on the stressed end syllables of rhymewords; generally considered to be stronger, more forceful than feminine rhymes.

EXAMPLES: *hand, land; ahead, abed.*

See FEMININE RHYME

maxim A brief, concise statement usually containing practical wisdom or advice.

EXAMPLES: "Haste makes waste." "A stitch in time saves nine."

See ADAGE, APHORISM, EPIGRAM, PROVERB

Marxism A set of doctrines concerning politics, sociology, and history. Projected by Karl Marx in his book *Das Kapital*, Marxism sees history as a class struggle between laboring and capitalistic classes and believes that all social actions and institutions are determined by economic considerations. Marxist literary critics have found economic struggles and determinations to be prominent in the literature of the 1930s.

EXAMPLES: Marxist critics have written extensively on the works of John Steinbeck and Upton Sinclair as well as on the earlier novels of Theodore Dreiser and Charles Dickens.

melodrama Although the term literally means "a play with music," melodrama today denotes a play with stereotyped characters and highly charged emotion, usually with a romantic plot and a happy ending. It is also used to describe a thrilling play that evokes horror. Thomas Holcroft's *A Tale of Mystery* (1802) is the first melodrama.

metaphor A figure of speech implying a comparison between objects of different classes or categories by saying one object *is* another, not *like* another.

EXAMPLES: "Bertram is a tiger when he gets angry." "His wife is a shrew." Notice that Bertram and his wife are humans, not wild animals, and therefore the implied comparisons are valid.

> *For secrets are edged tools,*
> *And must be kept from children and from fools.*
>
> > *Dryden*

See SIMILE

metonymy   A figure of speech in which a word that is closely associated with a term is substituted for the term itself.

EXAMPLE: "We insure you from the cradle to the grave." Here, *cradle* stands for birth, and *grave* stands for death.

> *Beneath the rule of men entirely great*
> *The pen is mightier than the sword.*
>
> > *Edward G. Bulwer-Lytton*

metrics   The branch of study of poetry that deals with patterns of rhythm and accent.

miracle play   A type of drama, common in medieval England, that depicts a miracle performed by a saint, or an incident in the life of one. These plays usually are not based strictly on scriptural accounts.

EXAMPLES: *Play of the Sacrament* (late 15th century), *Mary Magdalene* (*ca.* 1500).

See MYSTERY PLAY

mock epic   A long poem, intended to be humorous, that treats a trivial subject in the lofty and exalted style of the epic poem. The mock epic imitates and burlesques the traditions of the true epic.

EXAMPLES: Pope's *The Rape of the Lock* and Byron's *Don Juan*.

See BURLESQUE

monologue A discourse either oral or written by one speaker only; also called a soliloquy.

EXAMPLES: Many of the poems of Robert Browning, such as "My Last Duchess," are monologues; in that case, a dramatic monologue. Hamlet's speech beginning "To be, or not to be" is a famous soliloquy.

See DIALOGUE

mood The tone prevalent in a literary work.

EXAMPLES: The tone or mood of a poem may be somber, jolly, melancholy, etc. Milton's famous companion poems, "L'Allegro" and "Il Penseroso," are poems with strong contrasting moods.

morality play A type of drama, popular in medieval England, characterized by a pronounced use of allegory to point up a moral teaching. Abstractions like Conscience, Death, the Seven Sins, etc., appear as speaking persons, who are usually involved in a struggle for a human soul.

EXAMPLES: *Everyman* is the best-known medieval morality play; another is Skelton's *Magnificence*.

motivation The cause of action by a character in fiction or drama.

EXAMPLE: Macbeth's villainous murders are motivated by a lust for power and the urgings of an ambitious wife.

mystery play A type of medieval play based on Biblical stories, such as the sacrifice of Isaac, the death of Abel, the birth of Christ, and the trial and crucifixion of Jesus. These plays were the most important form of drama in the Middle Ages and continued to be popular into the Renaissance. They were most often performed in cycles associated with great cathedral towns: York, Chester, and Coventry.

See MIRACLE PLAY

mysticism The theory that some knowledge, such as the knowledge of God, can be received only by a means outside the human senses.

EXAMPLE: The works of William Blake, the 19th-century poet and engraver, reflect an intense mysticism.

myth Stories that come anonymously from the remote past; myths stir the subconscious in powerful ways because such folklore and folk beliefs are based on a kind of primitive truth that once explained inexplicable psychological and scientific truths to distant ancestors.

EXAMPLES: The myth of Prometheus attempts to explain how man received fire and the ability to use it; the myth of Pandora's box explains the cause of disorder in the world. In *Gulliver's Travels*, Swift uses a myth-like structure in recounting adventures in a land of giants or tiny persons.

naturalism A type of realistic fiction that developed in France, America, and England in the late 19th and early 20th centuries. It presupposes that human beings are like puppets, controlled completely by external and internal forces. Naturalism differs from realism in that characters in the latter have a measure of free will.

EXAMPLES: Emile Zola's *Nana*; Theodore Dreiser's *Sister Carrie* and *An American Tragedy*.

See REALISM

Neoclassicism A term used to describe a set of literary characteristics that flourished in the age between the Restoration (beginning in 1660) and the publication of *Lyrical Ballads* (1798), which signaled the triumph of romanticism in English literature. Neoclassical literature is characterized by a kind of elegance, wit, common sense, reason, and a careful control of emotions.

EXAMPLES: The poems in the heroic couplet by Dryden and Pope (either didactic or satirical).

See HEROIC COUPLET

New Criticism, the A school of literary criticism espoused by the critics John Crowe Ransom, Allen Tate, Robert Penn Warren, and Cleanth Brooks; the name comes from Ransom's book *The New Criticism* (1941). This type of literary criticism emphasizes a close analysis of the text of the work, which is considered complete in itself and independent of other works, with no historical and biographical contexts.

EXAMPLE: *Understanding Poetry*, by Brooks and Warren, is a handbook of the New Criticism.

See ANALYTICAL CRITICISM

nom de plume French for pen name; alias adopted by a writer to conceal his or her true identity.

EXAMPLES: George Eliot is the pen name of Mary Ann Evans; O. Henry, of William Sydney Porter.

novel A long narrative work of prose fiction that has characters and plot.

EXAMPLES: Novels are as varied as Melville's *Moby Dick*, Joyce's *Ulysses*, and Tolstoy's *War and Peace*.

novella A term frequently used to denote the early tales or short stories of French and Italian writers; a short novel.

EXAMPLES: The *Decameron* by Boccaccio; the *Heptameron* by Marguerite of Valois; and *The Aspern Papers* by Henry James.

objective correlative A literary term coined by T. S. Eliot to denote the technique of indirectly eliciting a desired emotional response from the reader through a pattern of objects, symbols, or events. The response is suggested rather than directly prescribed.

EXAMPLES: In Eliot's own works, *The Wasteland* demonstrates the use of the objective correlative:

> *April is the cruellest month, breeding*
> *Lilacs out of the dead land, mixing*
> *Memory and desire, stirring*
> *Dull roots with spring rain.*

occasional verse Poetry written for a special occasion, usually to honor royalty or to commemorate the death of a national hero.

EXAMPLES: Tennyson's "Ode on the Death of the Duke of Wellington"; Dryden's "Astraea Redux," written when Charles II returned to the throne.

octameter A line of poetry containing eight feet.

EXAMPLE: *Ă mán ĭn clóthĕs sŏ óld ănd thín
             ănd wórn ănd lápsĕd ĭn stýlĕ ănd tástĕ.*

octave A poetic stanza with eight lines; now primarily used to denote the first eight-line division of an Italian sonnet.

EXAMPLES: Longfellow's "Skeleton in Armor," E. A. Robinson's "For a Dead Lady." Octaves within Italian sonnets are found in Keat's "On First Looking into Chapman's Homer" and Mrs. Browning's sonnet "How Do I Love Thee?"

See ITALIAN SONNET

ode A sustained lyric poem with a noble theme and intellectual tone. There are three principal variations: the regular ode, or Pindaric Ode; the irregular ode, or Cowleyan Ode; and the Horatian Ode.

EXAMPLES: Shelley, "Ode to the West Wind"; Coleridge, "Ode to France"; and Collins, "Ode to Liberty."

See PINDARIC ODE, IRREGULAR ODE, HORATIAN ODE

omniscient point of view A way of telling a story that enables a fiction writer to enter the minds of his characters and reveal their inner thoughts while reporting external details and dialogue. The author can also comment on the meaning of the action.

EXAMPLES: Charles Dickens and George Eliot, two prolific novelists, use this method in most of their works.

See POINT OF VIEW

onomatopoeia A word whose sound suggests its sense or meaning. Such words add a vivid quality to poetry.

EXAMPLES: *hiss*, *clang*, *splash*, *buzz*, *murmur*.

ottava rima A poetic stanza with eight iambic pentameter lines rhyming *abababcc*. Supposedly invented by Boccaccio, it was used widely by Milton, Keats, and Byron.

EXAMPLE: *In her first passion woman loves her lover,*
In all the others all she loves is love,
Which grows a habit she can ne'er get over,
And fits her loosely—like an easy glove,
As you may find, whene'er you like to prove
    her:
One man alone at first her heart can move;
She then prefers him in the plural number,
Not finding that the additions much en-
    cumber.

                                          Byron

oxymoron A poetic device in which two words of opposite meaning are brought together in an emphatic way.

EXAMPLES: Shakespeare's "I know this is a joyful trouble to you." Milton's "bright darkness." Other examples are "wise fool," "generous miser" and "strong weakling."

palindrome A word or sentence that reads the same from left to right or right to left.

EXAMPLES: Hannah, pip; "Madam, I'm Adam"; "Able was I ere I saw Elba."

panegyric A written or oral composition that highly praises a person or place. In Greek literature panegyrics were most often for the dead; in Roman literature, for the living.

EXAMPLES: Gorgias, the *Olympiacus*; Pliny the Younger's speech praising Trajan.

parable A story told to illustrate a moral truth or lesson.

EXAMPLES: The Bible has the best-known parables: e.g., the sower, the prodigal son, the Good Samaritan.

pastoral A poem about shepherds and rural life, derived from ancient Greek poetry. The pastoral sometimes takes the form of a lament for a dead friend, a singing match between two shepherds, or a monologue. The word also can describe poetry marked by nostalgia for lost innocence.

EXAMPLES: Spenser's *The Shepheardes Calendar*, Vergil's *Eclogues*.

See PASTORAL ELEGY

pastoral elegy A serious poem written in an elevated, formal style and employing conventional pastoral imagery to commemorate the death of a friend, usually a poet.

EXAMPLES: Shelley's *Adonais*, Milton's *Lycidas*, Arnold's *Thyrsis*.

paronomasia An older and more elegant name for the play on words usually called a pun, which suggests or brings to mind a familiar word or phrase in a humorous way.

EXAMPLES: A young lady who drops out of college to marry is said to "put the heart before the course," a pun on the old saying, "put the cart before the horse." Another pun states that "a bun is the lowest form of wheat," a play on the saying, "a pun is the lowest form of wit."

See PUN

parody A humorous literary work that ridicules a serious work by imitating and exaggerating its style. A parody in literature is like a cartoon caricature.

EXAMPLES: Byron's "The Vision of Judgment" parodies Southey's poem of that name.

paradox A statement that appears to be absurd or self-contradictory but is true on a higher level; used for special emphasis in epigrams and similar writing.

EXAMPLES: "He who would save his life must lose it."
"None is so gullible as the unbeliever."

pathetic fallacy A phrase coined by the literary critic John Ruskin to describe poetic imagery that depicts things of nature as having the emotions of human beings. These images become a pathetic fallacy when they are absurd and overdone.

EXAMPLE: Ruskin often quoted the following:
They rowed her in across the rolling foam—
The cruel, crawling foam.
As Ruskin points out in *Modern Painters*, the foam is not cruel, nor does it crawl.

pentameter A line of poetry containing five metrical feet.

EXAMPLES: *Since all that beat about in Nature's range*
Or veer or vanish, why shouldn't thou re-
main
The only constant in a world of change
                                        Coleridge

See IAMBIC

periodic sentence A sentence in which the meaning is not complete until the end; usually in the pattern of a dependent clause followed by an independent clause; the opposite of a loose sentence. The purpose of the periodic sentence is to hold the reader's interest to the end and to add suspense.

EXAMPLE: "Because the other children were laughing and pointing at him, he ran away quickly."

See LOOSE SENTENCE

periphrasis A method of stating an idea in an indirect, excessively wordy manner. Literally translated, it means "roundabout speaking."

EXAMPLES: "The answer is in the negative" is a periphrasis for the word "no." The phrase "the year's penultimate month" is a periphrasis for "November."

personal essay A type of informal, autobiographical essay that is sometimes intimately self-revealing and usually written in a conversational, often humorous style.

EXAMPLES: Charles Lamb's "Old China," William Hazlitt's "My First Acquaintance with Poets."

See ESSAY, FORMAL ESSAY, INFORMAL ESSAY

persona In the criticism of fiction, the term is used to refer to the person through whom the narrative is told. The persona may narrate the story in the first person, but this is not always true. In all cases the persona is a "mask" through which the author speaks.

EXAMPLE: In *Huckleberry Finn* Huck is Mark Twain's persona, and Twain is thereby given the freedom to state ideas and points of view (about racism, for example) that he could not state without interjecting his own person.

See OMNISCIENT POINT OF VIEW

personification A figure of speech that gives human forms and characteristics to abstractions, ideas, animals, and other creatures.

EXAMPLES: When a country is spoken of as "she"; the idea that "Justice is blind." John Keats, in his "Ode on a Grecian Urn," personifies the urn as an "unravished bride."

See PATHETIC FALLACY

phenomenology A philosophical system that premises that objects have a reality and a meaning only in the consciousness of the person perceiving them. Therefore, to analyze a work of art accurately, the phenomenologist critic must carefully exclude all prejudgments or inferences that come from outside his own intuition. In other words, a work of art exists only as it appears in the mind of the viewer or reader.

EXAMPLES: Essays in literary criticism by Mikel Dufrenne, Gaston Backelard, and Georges Poulet.

philology In a general sense, the scientific study of language and literature. More narrowly, the term refers only to the study of language.

EXAMPLES: A philologist might study the use of kennings in Anglo-Saxon literature.

See KENNING

picaresque novel A type of novel whose structure is a loosely strung together series of incidents concerning a hero who is usually a clever rascal of little means but of endless wiles.

EXAMPLES: Daniel Defoe's *Moll Flanders*, Henry Fielding's *Jonathan Wild*, Mark Twain's *Huckleberry Finn*.

Pindaric ode The regular ode, divided into three parts: strophe, antistrophe, and epode; named for the Greek poet Pindar.

EXAMPLES: Pindar's series of Olympian odes and his Pythian odes.

See HORATIAN ODE, IRREGULAR ODE

Platonic criticism A type of literary criticism that judges a work according to its usefulness for non-artistic purposes, or its extrinsic value: e.g., whether or not the work has a moral or expresses an ideal.

Platonism A term that denotes the idealistic philosophical doctrines of Plato, whose ideas have influenced many English poets.

EXAMPLES: Doctrines of Platonism include the concepts that virtue is achieved only when mankind governs its conduct with reason; that the soul has had a previous existence in the ideal world before being born into this one; and that ideal love and beauty are synonymous with virtue and truth.

plot A planned series of incidents or actions invented by an author to give a story dramatic conflict and structure.

EXAMPLES: In a typical plotted story, a conflict is presented and increased through a series of complications until it reaches a climax, followed by a denouement, or resolution.

See CLIMAX, DENOUEMENT

poetic justice In a work of fiction (or in real life), an occurrence in which virtue is rewarded and/or vice is punished in an unusual and unexpected way.

EXAMPLES: In almost any Victorian novel, such as those of Dickens and Trollope, there is a happy ending achieved by poetic justice: e.g., in *Oliver Twist* when the villainous Sikes accidentally hangs himself while trying to escape.

poetic license A practice, sometimes used by poets, of violating a rule of pronunciation, rhyme, spelling, or normal word order to achieve a desired metrical pattern.

EXAMPLE: Robert Frost uses an inverted word order in the well-known opening line of his poem "Mending Wall": "Something there is that doesn't love a wall." To rime *divine* and *masculine* would be taking poetic license.

poetry That category of literature characterized by highly imaginative language selected and arranged to elicit a specific emotional response. Poets use meaning, sound, and rhythm to incorporate a concentrated depiction of experience.

point of view A phrase used in literary criticism to denote the vantage point from which an author presents the action in a work of fiction.

EXAMPLES: In the *first person* point of view, the author uses the pronoun *I*, and is part of the story.

In the *third person* point of view, the author anonymously chronicles the actions and dialogue of his characters. In the *omniscient point of view*, the author enters the minds of his characters, while taking a third person point of view.

See OMNISCIENT POINT OF VIEW

portmanteau words A phrase coined by Lewis Carroll to describe words made up of two existing words. The new word carries shades of both previous meanings.

EXAMPLES: *Smog* is a combination of the words *smoke* and *fog*. A *drizmal* day might be both *dismal* and *drizzly*.

In the poem "Jabberwocky," Carroll uses *slithy* to mean a combination of *lithe* and *slimy*. He also uses *mimsy* to denote both *flimsy* and *miserable*.

preface A brief introductory statement or essay at the beginning of a book that allows the author to introduce the work to the reader, to make acknowledgements, and to acquaint the reader with any special information needed to understand the purpose of the book.

EXAMPLES: Most serious non-fiction books have introductory prefaces. John Dryden and George Bernard Shaw wrote prefaces to their plays which were really extended essays on the background of their subject.

prelude A brief introductory poem placed before a lengthy poem or a lengthy section of a poem.

EXAMPLE: The prelude to James Russell Lowell's *The Vision of Sir Launfal.*

prologue An introductory speech that precedes plays to give the audience pertinent facts necessary for understanding the characters and action. Prologues are monologues delivered by an actor.

EXAMPLES: Most plays in the Restoration and 18th century had prologues, usually written by the authors of the plays, but sometimes written in rhyme by the author's fellow poets. The expository speeches of the stage manager in Thornton Wilder's play *Our Town* are like prologues except that they occur throughout the play, never like choruses in Greek dramas.

prose Generally, any written or spoken expression that is not in poetic, rhythmic patterns. Specifically, the term is applied to literature that is not poetry. *Prose* should not be used to refer to catalogs of things, lists of words, etc.

EXAMPLES: The Bible, the essays of Joseph Addison, and the novels of Ernest Hemingway—as diverse as these are—all exemplify prose.

prosody A word applied to the theory and principles of writing poetry and which especially pertains to forms of rhythmic, accented, and stanzaic patterns. *Poet's Handbook* by Clement Wood is a useful book on prosody.

See METRICS

protagonist The leading character, usually the hero or heroine, in a novel or play. The character the protagonist is in conflict with, usually the villain, is called the antagonist.

EXAMPLES: Hamlet is the protagonist of the play *Hamlet*; Jane Eyre, of the novel of that name.

proverb A brief statement of an important truth relevant to practical daily living. A proverb is usually an ancient statement, often carried down through oral tradition.

EXAMPLES: The Book of Proverbs of the Bible offers many, including, "Love not sleep, lest thou come to poverty" and "It is better to dwell in the wilderness, than with a contentious and angry woman."

See ADAGE, APHORISM, EPIGRAM

pseudonym A fictitious name used by an author to hide his or her identity.

EXAMPLES: Emily and Charlotte Brontë used the pseudonyms Ellis and Currer Bell in the early 19th century, when women authors were uncommon.

See NOM DE PLUME

psychoanalytical criticism The study of the motivations and actions of characters in drama or fiction. Critics of this school closely analyze symbols and language to find meanings that are either consciously or subconsciously intended.

EXAMPLES: Ernest Jones's study, *Hamlet and Oedipus*; Leslie Fiedler's *Love and Death in the American Novel*.

pun A play on words that employs the similarity of sounds between words of different meanings in a clever and unexpected way.

EXAMPLES: Thomas Hood's sentence: "They went and told the sexton and the sexton tolled the bell."

See PARONOMASIA

pure poetry A term applied to a poem written only for the beauty of its sound and imagery. It does not teach a moral truth or have conceptualized thoughts.

EXAMPLE: Edgar Allan Poe's poem "Annabel Lee" is pure poetry; this term was first used, in fact, by Baudelaire in an essay on Poe's poetry.

pyrrhic A poetic foot that has two unaccented syllables. Since there is no accented syllable, purists argue that the pyrrhic cannot be a true poetic foot.

EXAMPLE: Only in classical Latin and Greek poetry is the pyrrhic common. There is no English word without at least one accented syllable.

quatrain A stanza or a poem with four lines, with many possible rhyme schemes, including *abab, aabb,* *abba, aaba*, and *abcb*. The last scheme is called the ballad stanza.

EXAMPLE: *Gallants attend and hear a friend,*
Trill forth harmonious ditty,
Strange things I'll tell which late befell
In Philadelphia city.

Francis Hopkinson

See BALLAD STANZA

realism A term generally applied to any literature that is true to life. It is specifically applied to a movement in France, England, and America in the latter half of the 19th century, when novelists paid great attention to describing life as it really is. The realists were reacting against the unreal excesses and exaggerations of Romanticism.

EXAMPLES: The novels of Balzac in France, George Eliot in England, and William Dean Howells in America.

See NATURALISM

refrain A regularly repeated phrase or line of poetry that recurs frequently in a poem or balled, especially in old folk ballads and songs.

EXAMPLE: *Hark to an exiled son's appeal,*
Maryland!
My Mother State, to thee I kneel,
Maryland!
For life and death, for woe and weal,
Thy peerless chivalry reveal,
And gird thy beauteous limbs with steel,
Maryland, my Maryland!

James Ryder Randall

repetition A device used in writing poetry or prose in which an idea is repeated for emphasis.

EXAMPLE: *Cannon to the right of them,*
Cannon to the left of them
Cannon in front of them
Volleyed and thundered.

Tennyson

requiem A solemn chant or dirge; a prayer for the soul of the dead, sung at funerals. The word is from the the Latin phrase *Requiem aeternam dona eis, Domine* ("Give eternal rest to them, O Lord").

EXAMPLE: *Slow, slow, fresh fount, keep time with my*
salt tears;
Yet slower, yet, O faintly gentle springs!
List to the heavy part the music bears,
Woe weeps out her division, when she
sings,
Droop herbs and flowers;
Fall grief in showers;
Our beauties are not ours;
O, I could still,
Like melting snow upon some craggy hill,
Drop, drop, drop, drop,
Since nature's pride is, now, a withered
daffodil.

Ben Jonson

rhetorical criticism A type of literary criticism that analyzes the devices of rhetoric (the art of persuasion) used by an author to induce the reader to interpret the work as the author intends.

EXAMPLE: Rhetorical criticism is more easily understood if one uses it to analyze a political speech. Ask the question: "What devices does the speaker use to convince the listener that what he is saying is the only correct line of reasoning?"

rhyme A similarity or correspondence in the vowel sounds of two words that have differing consonantal sounds.

EXAMPLES: *Man* and *can* rhyme. *Rite* and *right* are not considered rhymes because the consonantal sounds preceding the vowel sounds are the same.

rhyme royal A type of stanza containing seven iambic pentameter lines and rhyming *ababbcc*. It is said to have received its royal name because James I of Scotland used the form.

EXAMPLE: *Thus he replies: "The colour in thy face*
             (That even for anger makes the lily pale,
             And the red rose blush at her own disgrace)
             Shall plead for me, and tell my loving tale:
             Under that colour am I come to scale
             Thy never-conquer'd fort: the fault is
                thine,
             For those thine eyes betray thee unto
                mine."

                                              Shakespeare

See IAMBIC, PENTAMETER

rhyme scheme The recurring pattern in which rhymes are placed in a stanza or poem. The pattern is normally indicated by using the letter *a* to indicate the first rhyme word, *b*, the second, and so on.

EXAMPLE: *There has fallen a splendid tear*   a
From the passion-flower at the gate.   b
She is coming, my dove, my dear;   a
She is coming, my life, my fate;   b
The red rose cries, 'She is near, she is
near;'   a
And the white rose weeps, 'She is late;'   b
The larkspur listens, 'I hear, I hear;'   a
And the lily whispers, 'I wait.'   b
                                              Tennyson

rising action That part of the plot of a story or drama in which the conflict between the hero or heroine (the protagonist) and the villain (the antagonist) becomes increasingly complicated.

EXAMPLE: In a story about a political candidate in a quest for the governor's office, the rising action would include all the increasing complications and obstacles in the candidate's path. In Hemingway's *The Old Man and the Sea* the rising action begins when the old man hooks the tremendous fish and the battle between man and behemoth begins.

roman à clef A novel based on real persons and events.

EXAMPLES: F. Scott Fitzgerald's *The Far Side of Paradise*; Ernest Hemingway's *The Sun Also Rises*.

See BILDUNGSROMAN

romance Originally a term denoting a medieval narrative in prose or poetry dealing with a knightly hero; but now, any fiction concerning heroes, exotic subjects, passionate love, or supernatural experiences.

EXAMPLES: *Sir Gawain and the Green Knight* (a medieval romance), Sir Walter Scott's *Rob Roy* and *Ivanhoe* (medieval romances written at a later time).

run-on line A line of poetry in which the sense of the sentence or clause is not completed (as in an end-stopped line) but which continue into a succeeding line.

EXAMPLE: *For I have revelled, when the sun was*
*   bright*
I' the summer sky, in dreams of living light
And loveliness,—have left my very heart
In climes of mine imagining, apart
From mine own own home, with beings that
*   have been*
Of mine own thought.

                                                          Poe

See END-STOPPED LINE

saga A prose narrative of heroic and legendary events in ancient Norway and Iceland; or any modern narrative that resembles Nordic sagas in style and subject matter.

EXAMPLES: "Grettir the Strong"; *Heimskringla*, from which Longfellow drew materials for his *Saga of King Olaf*.

satire A type of literary work that uses sarcasm, wit, and irony to ridicule and expose the follies and foibles of mankind, often in an attempt to reform society.

EXAMPLES: Alexander Pope's *The Rape of the Lock*, Jonathan Swift's *Gulliver's Travels*.

scansion The analysis of poetry or verse to show its metrical pattern.

EXAMPLE: A scansion of the line "Double, double, toil and trouble," from the incantation of the witches in *Macbeth*, would read: *Dóuble | dóuble | tóil and | tróuble*. The marks indicate there are four trochaic feet in the line.

See TROCHEE

scene A subdivision of an act of a play. In motion pictures a scene is a single situation or unit of dialogue.

EXAMPLES: In Shakespeare's time each act was divided into many scenes in different places. In modern dramas scene divisions are rare and are used primarily to show a brief passage of time.

See ACT

science fiction A form of fantasy in fiction in which scientific theories, hypotheses, and logic are used to create settings on other planets and galaxies and to depict the future on Earth.

EXAMPLES: Novels and short stories by Ray Bradbury and Ursula LeGuin are typical of the genre. Ms. LeGuin's *The Lathe of Heaven* explores the possibilities of using social as well as scientific speculation in science fiction.

semiotics The study of symbols and signs in works of literature.

EXAMPLES: A general study of symbols includes semantics (word meanings), syntactics (structural relationships among symbols), and pragmatics (the relationship between behavior and symbols).

See STRUCTURALISM

sestet A six-line stanza (also called a sextet) commonly found as the concluding six lines of a sonnet. The sestet is also used as a stanzaic form in itself and as a stanza in a poem.

EXAMPLE: *I wandered lonely as a cloud*
            That floats on high o'er vales and hills,
        When all at once I saw a crowd,
          A host, of golden daffodils;
              Beside the lake, beneath the trees,
              Fluttering and dancing in the breeze.
                                    Wordsworth

setting The physical background of a narrative. A setting includes the historical epoch in which the action occurs, as well as the social class or condition of the characters.

EXAMPLE: The setting for Margaret Mitchell's novel *Gone with the Wind* is the Deep South of the United States at the time of the Civil War, and the characters live highly gregarious lives on prosperous plantations.

short story A brief narrative, ancient in origin, which includes fables, parables, tales, and anecdotes. The short story as a conscious art form began to appear in the 19th century in the works of Hawthorne, Poe, and Balzac, whose short stories are carefully plotted and written for a calculated effect on the reader.

EXAMPLES: Poe's "The Fall of the House of Usher," "The Tell-Tale Heart," and "The Purloined Letter"; Hawthorne's "Young Goodman Brown" and "The Minister's Black Veil."

See NOVELLA

simile A figure of speech in which an object in one class is said to be like an object in another.

EXAMPLES: *My love is like a red, red rose.*
Burns

The poet compares his beloved to a flower. "His face was as red as a beet" indicates the degree of redness by comparing *face* with *beet*.

situation The set of circumstances in which the characters find themselves either at the beginning of or during the course of a story, novel, or drama. Many television series are based on the concept of the "situation comedy," in which characters are placed in a ridiculous situation for humorous effect.

EXAMPLE: The narrative of *Othello* derives from the following. A rough, military hero marries a beautiful, high-born lady; a subordinate, envious of the hero's stature, plants seeds of jealousy and distrust.

slant rhyme A term used to denote words that nearly rhyme. Often this occurs because of the substitution of assonance or consonance for true rhyme.

EXAMPLES: *molten* and *golden*; *hail* and *hole*.

See ASSONANCE, CONSONANCE

soliloquy A monologue delivered by an actor alone on stage. The intention of the speech is to reveal what is going on in the character's mind.

EXAMPLE: Probably the most famous is Hamlet's soliloquy, which begins, "To be, or not to be."

See MONOLOGUE

sonnet A poem of 14 iambic pentameter lines with a rigidly prescribed rhyme scheme. The two main types of sonnets are the Italian (or Petrarchan) and the English (or Shakespearean).

EXAMPLE:

> *When in disgrace with fortune and men's eyes,*
> *I all alone beweep my outcast state,*
> *And trouble deaf Heaven with my bootless cries,*
> *And look upon myself, and curse my fate,*
> *Wishing me like to one more rich in hope,*
> *Featur'd like him, like him with friends possess'd,*
> *Desiring this man's art, and that man's cope,*
> *With what I most enjoy contented least,*
> *Yet in these thoughts myself almost despising,*
> *Haply I think on thee—and then my state*
> *(Like to the lark at break of day arising*
> *From sullen earth) sings hymns at heaven's gate;*
> *For thy sweet love remember'd such wealth brings,*
> *That then I scorn to change my state with kings.*
>
> *Shakespeare*

See ITALIAN SONNET

Spenserian stanza A nine-line stanzaic form consisting of eight iambic pentameter lines followed by an Alexandrine, or a line of six iambic feet. The form was invented by Spenser and used in the 3,848 stanzas of *The Faerie Queen*. It rhymes *ababbcbcc*.

EXAMPLE:

> *Full on this casement shone the wintry moon,*
> *And threw warm gules on Madeline's fair*
> *   breast,*
> *As down she knelt for Heaven's grace and boon;*
> *Rose-bloom fell on her hands, together prest,*
> *And on her silver cross soft amethyst,*
> *And on her hair a glory, like a saint;*
> *She seem'd a splendid angel, newly drest,*
> *Save wings, for heaven:—Porphyro grew faint:*
> *She knelt, so pure a thing, so free from mortal*
> *   taint.*

> *Keats*

See ALEXANDRINE

spondee A type of poetic foot composed of two syllables, both of which are stressed.

EXAMPLES: Néw Yórk, wávelíke, cátlíke.

spoonerism An accidental and often humorous interchanging of the initial sounds of two or more words; named for Dr. W. A. Spooner of New College, Oxford, who often made such transpositions in his lectures.

EXAMPLES: A "well-boiled icicle" for a "well-oiled bicycle"; a "blushing crow" for a "crushing blow."

stanza A group of lines of poetry arranged as a melodic unit that follows a definite pattern. The number of lines in a stanza can vary from 2 to 12 (a few rare exceptions have even more).

EXAMPLE: The following stanza is a quatrain and rhymes *abab*.

Love seeketh not itself to please,
Not for itself hath any care,
But for another gives its ease,
And builds a Heaven in Hell's despair.
                                    William Blake

stock character A character that has become standard and customary in certain types of literature.

EXAMPLES: A cruel stepmother and a Prince Charming are stock characters of fairy tales; fainting heroines, of sentimental novels; disguised heroines and talkative old men, of Elizabethan drama.

stock response A response that is traditional and expected from the reader.

EXAMPLES: References to the flag or to motherhood call for stock responses.

stream-of-consciousness novel A type of psychological novel that presents the inner thoughts of a character in an uneven, endless stream (or flow) that simulates the character's consciousness.

EXAMPLES: Virginia Woolf's *To the Lighthouse*, William Faulkner's *The Sound and the Fury*, and James Joyce's *Ulysses*.

stress The accent or emphasis given to a syllable or word in poetry or other rhythmic writing.

EXAMPLES: The words *about*, *beyond*, and *detain* stress the second syllables; *carry*, *daily*, and *greatly* stress the first syllable.

strophe A special designation for a stanza; in Pindaric odes the strophe is the first stanza and every subsequent third stanza (fourth, seventh, etc.).

See ANTISTROPHE, EPODE

structuralism A critical modern movement, originating in France, that studies literature, particularly fiction, from the point of view of its underlying system of language (structural linguistics) and its underlying anthropological system as manifested in the cultural phenomena of the work (structural anthropology).

EXAMPLES: The works of Ferdinand de Saussure deal with structural linguistics; those of Claude Levi-Strauss deal with structural anthropology.

sublime, the A quality in a literary work that is said to cause the reader to be transported out of himself to a lofty plane. In past literary periods, poets attained this sought-after goal by nobility and grandeur of style.

EXAMPLES: Works that are generally considered to have attained the sublime are Dante's *Divine Comedy*, Shakespeare's plays, Milton's *Paradise Lost*, and Goethe's *Faust*.

subplot A secondary dramatic conflict that runs through a story as a subordinate complication and which is less important than the main plot.

EXAMPLE: In Shakespeare's play, Hamlet's conflict with Laertes is a subplot.

symbol Something that is a meaningful entity in itself and yet stands for, or means, something else. In literature there are so-called universal symbols and others that suggest special meanings because of the way they are used in a novel or other literary work.

EXAMPLES: A flag, which is a symbol for a particular country; a voyage, a universal symbol for life. The scarlet letter in Hawthorne's novel assumes a special literary symbolism to those who know the novel thoroughly. Standing for the first letter in the world *Adultery*, the mark of shame gradually becomes a symbol of the bigotry and oppressive puritanism of a society.

symbolism A literary movement in France in the latter part of the 19th century which was influenced by Edgar Allan Poe. Symbolists believed that unique and highly personal emotional responses, conveyed to the reader by means of a system of subjective symbols, were the main substance of literature.

EXAMPLES: Works of the French writers Mallarmé, Rimbaud, and Baudelaire abound in this kind of symbolism. Baudelaire held that man lives in a "forest of symbols."

synaesthesia The describing of one kind of sensation in terms of another. For example, one can describe a sensation that comes through tactile feeling in terms of a sensation that comes through hearing.

EXAMPLES: The device is used often by Poe and by Dame Edith Sitwell, whose poem "Still Falls the Rain" has this synaesthetic image: "a sound like the pulse of the heart."

synecdoche A type of metaphor in which a part is

used to suggest a whole, or a whole to suggest a part.

EXAMPLES: "Sixty sails were in Her Majesty's fleets"; "Fifty winters passed him by" (one season suggests an entire year).

tail-rhyme stanzas Stanzas of poetry that contain two or more short lines rhyming together to serve as "tails" to the various parts of the stanza; called *rime couée* in French poems, *Schweifreim* in German stanzas.

EXAMPLE: *Wee, sleekit, cow-rin', tim'rous beastie,*
O what a panic's in thy breastie!
Thou need na start awa sae hasty,
Wi' bickering brattle;
I wad be laith to rin and chase thee
Wi' murd'ring pattle!

Burns

tale A simple story in prose or poetry. It is also used to denote an oral narrative, as in a "tall tale." The term can be used so generally that it is a part of Dickens's title for the novel *A Tale of Two Cities*, but it suggests a much shorter story, such as one of the tales of Uncle Remus by Joel Chandler Harris.

tercet A stanza of poetry with three lines. The most common rhyme schemes of the tercet are *aaa*, *aba*, *aab*, and *abb*.

EXAMPLE: *This truth within thy mind rehearse,*
That in a boundless universe
Is boundless better, boundless worse.

Tennyson

terza rima A special type of tercet that has interlocking rhymes in a continuous rhyme scheme: *aba bcb cdc ded*, etc.

EXAMPLE:

> *O wild West Wind, thou breath of Autumn's*
> *   being,*
> *Thou, from whose unseen presence the leaves dead*
> *Are driven, like ghosts from an enchanter fleeing,*
>
> *Yellow, and black, and pale, and hectic red,*
> *Pestilence-stricken multitudes: O thou,*
> *Who chariotest to their dark wintry bed*
>
> *The wingéd seeds, where they lie cold and low,*
> *Each like a corpse within its grave, until*
> *Thine azure sister of the Spring shall blow*
>
> *   Shelley*

tetrameter A line of poetry with four poetic feet.

EXAMPLE: *Behold her, single in the field,*
Yon solitary highland lass.

> *   Wordsworth*

(These lines are in iambic tetrameter.)

See IAMBIC

textual criticism An activity in which a literary scholar seeks to reconstruct an original manuscript and establish the authoritative text of the literary work.

EXAMPLES: This process could involve a close study of an original manuscript or, if that is lost, a conjecture based on the various versions of the printed text.

theme A central idea in a literary work; usually suggested by the narrative action.

EXAMPLES: A story might suggest the theme that goodness is its own reward, or that virtue always triumphs, or, more somberly, that "nice guys finish last."

tone The author's attitude toward his subject and his audience as implied in the literary work.

EXAMPLES: A literary tone may be, among other possibilities, formal, solemn, sarcastic, informal, satirical, playful, jocular, serious, etc.

tragedy A serious drama, in prose or poetry, about a person, often of a high station in life, who experiences sudden personal reversals and which ends with a catastrophic event.

EXAMPLES: Sophocles's *Antigone*; Shakespeare's *Hamlet* and *King Lear*; and Arthur Miller's *The Death of a Salesman*.

tragic force The incident or event in a tragic drama that triggers an action that results in the hero's downfall.

EXAMPLE: In Shakespeare's *Macbeth* the escape of Fleance marks the beginning of the catastrophic end of the hero, Macbeth.

tragic irony A form of irony that occurs when a character in a tragedy uses words that mean one thing to him and something more meaningful to those who are listening.

EXAMPLE: When Oedipus vows to find the murderer of his father, he doesn't know that he himself is the murderer.

tragi-comedy A type of drama that is initially serious in tone or theme, until it becomes apparent that the tragic events will end happily rather than with a catastrophic event.

EXAMPLE: Shakespeare's *The Merchant of Venice* ends without Shylock exacting his "pound of flesh," which would have been tragic for Antonio.

transcendentalism A belief that human beings may learn higher truths in ways that transcend the senses, including intuition and mysticism.

EXAMPLES: The writings of Emerson and Thoreau, in America; Coleridge, in England; and Goethe, in Germany.

See MYSTICISM

trilogy A literary work with three parts, each a complete unit.

EXAMPLES: John Dos Passos's *USA*, Shakespeare's *King Henry VI*.

trimeter A line of poetry containing three metrical feet.

EXAMPLES: Typical iambic trimeter lines would be:
> Then come, my love, to me....
> The glory of his death....
> The last immortal noon....

triolet A French verse form that has the first two lines of the eight-line stanza repeated as the last two lines, and the first line repeated as the fourth line.

EXAMPLE: *All women born are so perverse,*
No man need boast their love possessing,
If nought seems better, nothing's worse;
All women born are so perverse,
From Adam's wife that proved a curse
Though God had made her for a bless-
ing.
All women born are so perverse,
No man need boast their love possessing.

Bridges

triple rhyme   A rhyme in which three syllables in one word rhyme with three syllables of another.

EXAMPLES: *ascendancy, dependency; triolet, violet.*

trochee   A metrical foot with a stressed syllable followed by an unstressed syllable.

EXAMPLES: *Bóstŏn, áccĕnt.*

Why so pale and wan, fond lover?
Prithee, why so pale?
Will, when looking well can't move her,
Looking ill prevail?

Suckling

understatement   A form of irony, also called litotes, in which something is represented as less than it really is, with the intent of drawing attention to and emphasizing the opposite meaning.

EXAMPLES: "Helen of Troy was not a bad-looking woman." "Hercules was not exactly a weakling." e.e. cummings, in a well-known poem, says "Buffalo Bill's defunct" (rather than saying he is dead).

See LITOTES

unities Principles of structuring drama requiring the plot to be one continuous action (unity of action) that takes place within the walls of one city (unity of place) in one day (unity of time).

EXAMPLES: The only unity included in Aristotle's classic guide *Poetics* was that of action. Seventeenth- and 18th-century critics added others, in the belief that subplots destroyed unity of action and that mixing tragedy and comedy (as Shakespeare did) destroyed dramatic unity.

universality A characteristic of great literature, which are works of art that appeal to people in all countries in all eras.

EXAMPLES: Works of literature that achieve universality usually are those that illuminate an important facet of human nature, as in King Lear's failure to understand his daughters. Human nature, precisely delineated, is unchanging.

vers de société A sophisticated, playful verse—sometimes called light verse—usually on the foibles of social relationships and conventions.

EXAMPLES: Although this form has existed since the days of classical Greece, it was at its most popular in England in the 17th and 18th centuries and in the Victorian period.

> *Still to be neat, still to be dressed,*
> *As you were going to a feast;*
> *Still to be powdered, still perfumed;*
> *Lady, it is to be presumed,*
> *Though art's hid causes are not found,*
> *All is not sweet, all is not sound.*
> *Give me a look, give me a face*

> *That makes simplicity a grace,*
> *Robes loosely flowing, hair as free;*
> *Such sweet neglect more taketh me*
> *Then all th' adulteries of art.*
> *They strike mine eyes, but not my heart.*
> *Ben Jonson*

verse A general name given to all metrical (or poetic) compositions. Used specifically, the word mean a line of poetry or the stanza of a song; used generally, it suggests a lower order of poetry.

versification The making of verses; also used as a synonym for prosody to denote all the elements of poetic composition. In the latter sense, versification includes accent, rhythm, meter, rhyme, stanza form, etc.

See PROSODY

vers libre Another word for free verse, or poetry without a regular pattern of meter or rhyme.

EXAMPLE:

> *Or do my eyes misrepresent? Can this be he,*
> *That heroic, that renowned,*
> *Irresistible Samson? whom, unarmed,*
> *No strength of man, or fiercest wild beast, could*
> *   withstand;*
> *Who tore the lion as the lion tears the kid;*
> *Ran on embattled armies clad in iron,*
> *And, weaponless himself,*
> *Made arms ridiculous, useless the forgery*
> *Of brazen shield and spear, the hammered cuirass,*
> *Chalybean-tempered steel, and frock of mail*
> *Adamantean proof.*
> *Milton*

PART II
LANGUAGE SKILLS

abbreviation A shortened form of a word used for brevity in writing.

EXAMPLES: Some words, such as *Mister*, are almost always abbreviated. Other standard abbreviations are *Mrs.*, *Ms.*, *Dr.*, and *Prof.* Abbreviations also are used with certain dates and numerals (B.C., A.D., A.M., and P.M.) and in addresses and footnotes. One normally spells out personal names; the names of countries or states; the names of days, months, and holidays; and the names of courses of instruction (avoid Eng. Lit., for instance).

absolute phrase A phrase that modifies all words in a sentence rather than a single word or word group, and which does not have a connective joining it to the sentence. It is "absolute" in its function.

EXAMPLES: "The rainstorm being over, we started the car again." The opening phrase in the sentence is absolute. The following initial phrase is *not* absolute because it modifies *we*: "Seeing the washed-out bridge, we stopped the car."

abstract noun A noun that designates intangibles, such as qualities or ideas. Avoid the overuse of undefined abstract nouns.

EXAMPLES: *love*, *liberty*, *truth*.

acknowledgement of sources In any essay or other composition requiring the use of information from sources other than one's own knowledge, the sources must be listed so that one is not charged with plagiarism. Sources may be acknowledged by a clear reference in the body of the composition or in a footnote.

See FOOTNOTE, PLAGIARISM

acronym An abbreviation of the name of a governmental agency or bureau. An acronym differs from other abbreviations in that it can be pronounced as a word.

EXAMPLES: UNESCO (United Nations Educational, Scientific, and Cultural Organization) and SEATO (South-East Asia Treaty Organization). CARE is an acronym, but FBI is not. Notice that periods are not used in these abbreviations.

See ABBREVIATION

active voice The form of the verb that indicates the subject of a sentence is acting and not being acted upon. Only transitive verbs can show active (or passive) voice.

EXAMPLE: "The lion mauled the hunter." If it were stated: "The hunter was mauled by the lion," the sentence would be passive. Avoid the excessive use of the passive voice, which can result in weak sentences.

See TRANSITIVE VERBS, PASSIVE VOICE

addresses, in business letters The conventional form for writing addresses in business letters and on envelopes is the block form. Note that an abbreviated title such as Mr., Ms., or Mrs. usually should be placed before the name.

EXAMPLE: Ms. Dawn Early, Editor
Aurora Magazine
230 E. 43rd Street
New York, N.Y. 10016

adjective A word that modifies nouns or pronouns. Adjectives have three forms: Positive: *hot* climate;

Comparative: the *hotter* climate of two cities; Superlative: the *hottest* climate of any city. Adjectives like *famous* have no comparative or superlative forms; use "*more famous* of the two" and "the *most famous* of all."

EXAMPLES: *blue* skies, *poor* me (descriptive); *two* thieves, *only* her (limiting).

adjective clause A clause that modifies a noun or pronoun.

EXAMPLES: "The man *whom they saw* was red-haired." "The road *that they traveled* was rocky." The *italicized* clauses modify *man* and *road*.

adjective phrase A phrase that modifies a noun or pronoun.

EXAMPLES: "The girl *with the torn skirt* is Debbie." "I like the one *on the top shelf*." The underlined adjective phrases modify *girl* and *one*. Notice that the phrases, which begin with the prepositions *on* and *with*, are prepositional phrases that function as adjective phrases.

See PREPOSITIONAL PHRASE

adverb A word that modifies verbs, adjectives, and other adverbs. Adverbs show degrees of quality or quantity and have three forms:
Positive: *quickly*;
Comparatively: *more quickly*;
Superlative: *most quickly*.
Some adverbs retain old irregular forms: *badly*, *worse*, *worst*.

EXAMPLES: run *swiftly*, *very* pretty, *quite well* co-ordinated.

adverb clause A dependent, or subordinate, clause that functions in a sentence as an adverb to indicate time, place, cause, result, etc.

EXAMPLES: 1. "*When you come*, bring a bucket of ice." The *italicized* clause modifies the verb *bring*. 2. "The best mushrooms were found *where the creek crossed the meadow*." The *italicized* clause modifies *were found*.

See CLAUSE

adverb phrase A phrase that functions in a sentence as an adverb to indicate time, place, cause, result, etc.

EXAMPLES: 1. "The quarterback ran *across the goal line*." The *italicized* phrase modifies *ran*. 2. "She waited *until three o'clock*." The *italicized* phrase modifies *waited*.

See PHRASE

agreement The matching of the form of a noun with its verb and a pronoun with its antecedent.

EXAMPLES: A subject and verb must agree in number and person: "They *go* each day" is correct. "They *goes* each day" is not because a singular verb is used with a plural subject. A pronoun must agree with its antecedent (the noun or pronoun to which it refers) in person, number, and gender: "She wanted *her* way," not "she wanted *their* way" or "*his* way."

See ANTECEDENT

ampersand A character (&) that stands for the word *and*.

EXAMPLES: The ampersand may be used in addresses

and footnotes, but rarely in formal writing: For instance, "Simon & Schuster" is acceptable for addressing an envelope, but "Simon and Schuster" is preferred in a letter or formal text.

analogy A method of developing an essay or paragraph by comparing one process, action, or object to another that is similar.

EXAMPLE: You could write an essay on your first year in college by comparing it to a ride on a roller coaster.

analysis A method of developing a paragraph or a complete essay by describing the parts of the object being discussed.

EXAMPLES: A botanist writing an analysis of an apple would analyze it into stem, flesh, seeds, etc.

antecedent A noun, pronoun, or group of nouns or pronouns to which a pronoun refers.

EXAMPLES: "*John* came early, but *he* stayed quite late." *John* is the antecedent of *he*.

See AGREEMENT

antonym A word that has the opposite meaning of another.

EXAMPLES: *Light* is an antonym for *dark*, *joy* for *sadness*, etc.

See SYNONYM

apostrophe A character (') used to indicate the possessive case of nouns and indefinite pronouns and to indicate that a letter has been left out in contractions.

EXAMPLES: *boy's* tricycle (plural, *boys'* tricycle); *who's* (contraction for who is); *everyone's* need (indefinite pronoun, possessive case).

appositive A grammatical construction in which one or more words or phrases, usually adjacent, refer to the same person or thing.

EXAMPLES: "*my brother* Wesley" or "Wesley, *my brother*"; "*his sport*, football."

archaic words Words that are old-fashioned and out of date; rarely used in general, informal writing.

EXAMPLES: *forsooth, belike, hark.*

argumentation The act or process of reasoning and drawing a conclusion in a written or oral composition or debate. Its purpose is to resolve a conflict or disagreement and/or to persuade another person to accept a new point of view.

EXAMPLES: Many essays and compositions are basically arguments; for example, an essay might be written on "Why we should support our sports teams." Political debates contain argumentation, as do some letters to the editor and some television editorials.

argumentum ad hominem A type of false reasoning, literally translated as "argument against the man." This fallacy occurs when one attacks the person making the argument rather than the argument itself.

EXAMPLE: I haven't read George's argument, and I don't need to. He's one of the biggest radicals in town, and I know we won't agree with him.

article A word that traditionally has been called a limiting adjective but which modern grammarians refer to as a "determiner" because it always signals that a noun will follow.

EXAMPLES: *A* and *an* are indefinite articles, and *the* is the definite article.

attributive adjective An adjective that is positioned either immediately before or immediately after the word it modifies.

EXAMPLES: *red* fox, attorney *general*, *faulty* key, court *martial*.

auxiliary verb A verb form used with a main verb to make a verb phrase.

EXAMPLES: One group of auxiliary verbs is used to indicate tense and voice: *shall go, has gone, does go.* The other group indicates obligation, ability, possibility, etc.: *could go, may go, might go,* etc.

balanced sentence A compound or compound-complex sentence that has parallel coordinate clauses. Less commonly, the term is applied to sentences that have parallel parts, clauses, or phrases. The effect of a balanced sentence is increased emphasis.

EXAMPLES: 1. In the 1950s Americans attempted to keep up with the Joneses; in the 1980s they attempted to keep up with technological change. 2. The girl scouts were stranded without matches, without warm clothing, and without a tent.

See COMPOUND SENTENCE, COMPOUND-COMPLEX SENTENCE, COORDINATE CLAUSE

bandwagon fallacy A type of faulty argument in which a speaker or writer appeals to one's natural preference for being on the winning side by making an unwarranted assumption as to which side will win. People who join a political party late, when it is clear that the party is winning, are said to be jumping on the bandwagon.

EXAMPLE: "Everyone is supporting Senator Blank; you'd better get on the winning team."

begging the question A type of fallacy in logic in which a part of what has to be proved in an argument is simply assumed to be true without proof.

EXAMPLE: "The Supreme Court gives the common criminal too much advantage over policemen. When a person is arrested by the police, he should not have any rights." Begged question: the assumption that all persons arrested have committed a crime; the jury must decide this. It also assumes that the Bill of Rights applies only to certain persons.

bibliography A listing of books, periodicals, and other sources used in the writing of a research paper, term paper, or other scholarly work.

EXAMPLES: There is a strict form to be followed in a bibliography. Consult your textbook or your teacher for the specific form required. Typical entries include:
Hawkins, Edward. *Stargazing*. Chicago: Rack and
    Ruin, Inc., 1981.
Wrench, Wanda. "Head for the Stars," *Spyglass*, 21
    (November, 1982), 27–31.

See FOOTNOTES

brackets Characters ([ ]) used within quotations to separate one's own comments from the words of the writer or speaker being quoted.

EXAMPLE: "The outside linebacker [Pete Savage] played a fantastic game," Coach Bryant said.

business letter A letter written for the purpose of applying for a job, asking for a refund, complaining of poor service, or for many other reasons. A proper business letter should be straight-forward, as brisk as possible, grammatically correct, and, above all, clear in meaning.

EXAMPLE:

49 Premier Street
Atlanta, GA 30210
January 1, 1985

Ms. Shirley Surely, Manager
The Kitty Boutique
48 Catnip Avenue
Atlanta, GA 30209

Dear Ms. Surely:

When I purchased a bed for my cat on December 24, I was assured by one of your salespersons that my cat Jacques would love the bed, would sleep on it every night, and would welcome it as a gift appropriate to the season. Jacques not only has never slept on the bed, he will not even go near it. He continues to sleep curled up on the top edge of the back of an overstuffed chair.

Since this product was misrepresented to me, I would like a full refund of my purchase price, including sales tax. Please call me at 830-7411 at your convenience to advise me as to how the refund will be made.

Sincerely,

George Spaniel

capitalization The practice of using a capital letter to indicate proper nouns and adjectives, the first word in a sentence or in a line of poetry, and significant words in titles of books, plays, etc. Capitalize the first word in a title and all other words except articles, prepositions, and conjunctions that have fewer than five letters.

EXAMPLES: 1. "Be careful!" 2. *Gone with the Wind*.

case A word denoting the form of a pronoun or noun. This special form indicates the function of the pronoun or noun in the sentence.

EXAMPLES: Pronouns:
1. nominative case (used as a subject): *we*, *I*, *she*;
2. possessive case (as an adjective): *my* cap, *your* glove;
3. objective case (used as objects of verbs, verbals, and prepositions): *them*, *us*, *him*.
Nouns:
1. Common case, *boy*, *girl*; 2. possessive case, *boy's*, *girl's*.

cause and effect analysis A method of developing a paragraph or an essay by answering one of the following questions: "What caused this?" or "Given this set of circumstances, what effect will follow?"

EXAMPLES: One could write a brief essay on why milk turns to yogurt or why animals age on a chronological scale different from humans.

central idea The principal thesis of an essay, often stated as a topic sentence at the beginning of an outline. The central idea includes the scope of the essay as well as an indication of how the author will treat the material.

EXAMPLE: The protest against the Vietnam War, as it increased in the last months of the war, came to include people of all ages and social conditions.

See THESIS SENTENCE, TOPIC SENTENCE

circumlocution A sentence that uses too many words to say what is better said directly.

EXAMPLE: Every person who does any thinking at all these days seems to agree with the conception that the world is in a great deal of trouble. (Today every thinking person seemingly agrees that the world is in trouble.)

classification A method of developing a paragraph or an essay by organizing information into groups or classes according to a principle of selection. In an ideal classification all items should fit into a category and no items should be left out.

EXAMPLES: If you were classifying types of trees you would divide them into two groups: those that shed their leaves (deciduous) and those that do not. Then you would go into a number of subclassifications.

clause A group of words containing a subject and a predicate.

EXAMPLES: Main clauses can stand independently: "The fast train roared down the track." Subordinate clauses depend on other sentence elements for completeness: "When the fast train roared down the track, the horses were frightened."

clichés Words and phrases that are trite and so overused they have become almost meaningless.

EXAMPLES: *slow but sure*, *cool as a cucumber*.

coherence A characteristic of good writing that makes it easy for the reader to see relationships between one thought and another, one sentence and another, one paragraph and another. Coherence in a paragraph can be achieved in the following ways: (1) the logical, orderly arrangement of sentences; (2) repeating key words and using pronouns to refer to preceding sentences; (3) using transitional expressions; and (4) using parallel structure.

See PARALLELISM, TRANSITIONAL EXPRESSIONS

collective noun A type of noun that uses a singular form to name a group of individuals or things.

EXAMPLES: *team*, *jury*, *congress*.
A singular verb is used when the collective noun denotes a group thought of as a unit: "The jury is out." A plural verb is used when the individuals in the group are denoted: "The family were notified by telephone."

colloquialism A conversational word, phrase, or construction that is appropriate in informal speech and writing, but inappropriate in formal, literary settings. Some dictionaries indicate words that are colloquial.

EXAMPLES: *awfully* (meaning "very"); *cute*; *over with* (meaning "completed"); *sort of*.

colon A punctuation mark (:) used after a word that introduces a quotation, a list of items, or a summary. It is also used after the salutation of a formal letter (Dear Mr. Verdi:).

EXAMPLES: 1. Sir William Gilbert wrote: "Spurn not the nobly born with love affected, nor treat with virtuous scorn the well-connected." 2. Bring the following supplies: cooking oil, salt, and pepper. 3. The facts lead me to conclude one thing: she could not have been on the street corner at that particular time.

comma A punctuation mark (,) used to indicate the separation of elements or of ideas within a sentence and to set off non-restrictive modifiers.

EXAMPLES: 1. "We need to buy tea, biscuits, and milk." The separation of items in a series. 2. "Debra went to the theater, and George stayed home to watch television." The separation of independent clauses joined by the coordinating conjunction *and*. 3. "He was not, you know, the smartest player on the team." The separation of parenthetical elements. 4. "Casey, my friend, is going." The setting off of non-restrictive modifiers.

comma splice An error in sentence structure in which two independent clauses are put together with a comma joining, or splicing, them.

EXAMPLE: "He preferred fried eggs, he got scrambled eggs." This sentence can be corrected by using a semicolon instead of a comma.

comparison A term denoting the change in the form of adjectives and adverbs to show degree.
There are three forms of comparison:
Positive: *heavy*, *rapidly*, *good*;
Comparative: *heavier*, *more rapidly*, *better*;
Superlative: *heaviest*, *most rapidly*, *best*.

EXAMPLES: Use the comparative form with two: "He was the heavier of the twins." Use the superlative form with more than two: "He was the heaviest of the three brothers."

complement A word that completes the sense of the predicate (a direct and/or indirect object), subject (a subject complement), or object (an object complement).

EXAMPLES: 1. Verb complement: "Give the devil his due." *Devil* is the indirect object; *due* is the direct object. 2. Subject complement: "I am a football fan." *Fan* complements the subject *I*. 3. Object complement: "I'll keep the cheerleaders happy." *Happy* complements the direct object *cheerleaders*.

complete predicate A group of words that includes the simple predicate (the verb and its auxiliaries) and any modifiers, complements, or objects related to the verb.

EXAMPLE: "A more experienced person *would have solved the problem immediately*." The italicized words make up the complete predicate; the simple predicate is *would have solved*.

complete subject A group of words that includes the simple subject and all its modifiers.

EXAMPLE: "*The old gray mare* is definitely not what she used to be." *Mare* is the simple subject; the words preceding it are modifiers.

complex sentence
A sentence containing one main clause and at least one subordinate clause.

EXAMPLE: "If we can control their passing attack, *we will win the game.*" The main clause, which is a complete sentence, is italicized.

compound adjective
An adjective made up of two or more words.

EXAMPLES: *run-of-the-mill*, *downcast*.

compound-complex sentence
A sentence that contains at least two main clauses and at least one subordinate clause.

EXAMPLE: I am watching this television program because you asked me to watch it, but I would much rather read a book.

compound noun
A noun made up of more than one word but used as a unit.

EXAMPLES: *basketball*, *redhead*, *booby trap*, *fathers-in-law*, *passersby*. Notice that the latter two compound nouns are given in the plural to show that the *s* is added to the noun.

compound predicate
Two or more verbs functioning equally in a sentence.

EXAMPLE: They *washed* and *waxed* the car in one afternoon.

compound sentence A sentence containing at least two main, or independent, clauses.

EXAMPLE: I have always enjoyed reading novels, but recently my interest has turned to non-fiction works of history and biography.

See INDEPENDENT CLAUSE

compound subject Two or more subjects functioning equally in a sentence.

EXAMPLE: *Tom* and *Harry* had a great time at the game.

conciseness The use of economy in constructing sentences so that no superfluous words, or circumlocutions, are used.

EXAMPLE: Of the two following sentences, only the second is concisely written: 1. "There is only one excuse that is acceptable, and that is 'I have no money.'" 2. "Only one excuse is acceptable: 'I have no money.'"

See CIRCUMLOCUTION

concrete noun A noun that names things that are tangible, as opposed to those that are abstract.

EXAMPLES: *jewels*, *coins*, *eggs*, *dogs*.

conjugation A listing of the forms of a verb that shows tense, voice, mood, person, and number.

EXAMPLE: The conjugation of the word *believe* in the present tense, active voice, indicative mood is *I believe, you believe, he/she/it believes, we believe, you believe, they believe.*

conjunction A word that links and relates two parts of a sentence.

EXAMPLES: *And*, *or*, *but*, *nor*, *for* are coordinating conjunctions; *either ... or* is a correlative conjunction; *after*, *although*, *as if*, *because* are subordinating conjunctions.

conjunctive adverb An adverb that joins two main clauses in a sentence.

EXAMPLES: "We hoped to take a ride in the country to see the autumn leaves; *however*, our car would not start." Other conjunctive adverbs are *also*, *besides*, *consequently*, *indeed*, and *therefore*. Notice that it is necessary to use a semicolon before these adverbs to avoid a comma splice.

See COMMA SPLICE

connotation The associations a word carries with it, as opposed to its literal meaning, or denotation.

EXAMPLES: Words like *home* and *horse* have generally favorable connotations, whereas *shack* and *nag* have unfavorable connotations.

See DENOTATION

consonants Speech sounds created by the partial or complete restriction of the air stream by the tongue, teeth, or palate, or by other constrictions of the speech organs. The letters corresponding to these sounds are *b*, *c*, *d*, *f*, *g*, *j*, *k*, *m*, etc.

See VOWELS

contractions Words that have been shortened; apostrophes are used to indicate missing letters.

EXAMPLES: *she'll* for *she will*, *don't* for *do not*.

contrast A method of developing a paragraph or an essay by showing how two persons, places, things, or ideas are different.

EXAMPLES: An essay showing contrast could be written on the following topics: big cities vs. small towns; my world and the world my parents knew as children; hawks and doves.

coordinate adjectives Two or more adjectives that modify the same noun or pronoun.

EXAMPLES: 1. The *bright* and *shiny* bauble delighted the children. 2. The *dark*, *damp* cave was spooky.

coordination The act of putting two or more elements of a sentence in the same order or rank.

EXAMPLES: 1. "John went to the theatre, and Alice stayed home." These two clauses are coordinated. 2. "When John went to the theatre, Alice stayed home." The first clause is subordinated, or a dependent clause.

coordinating conjunction A type of conjunction (a linking word) that connects main clauses.

EXAMPLES: *and*, *or*, *nor*, *but*, and, sometimes, *yet*, *so*, and *for*. Notice that a comma comes before the coordinating conjunction, as in the sentence: "It was cold and rainy, *and* the little boy was ready to go home."

correlative conjunctions Coordinating conjunctions that are used in pairs to join sentence elements of equal rank.

EXAMPLES: *not only ... but also*; *both ... and*; *either ... or*; *neither ... nor*. 1. She was not only the most beautiful person in the class, but also the most intelligent. 2. Both the pasta and the salad were delicious.

dangling modifier A group of words that is not linked to the word it modifies and therefore confusing to the reader.

EXAMPLES: "*Having eaten all the main dish*, the dinner was obviously enjoyed immensely." "*Bored by the one-sided score*, the stadium began to empty."

dash A character (—) used to show a sudden change in thought or an unfinished thought. Dashes can also be used to emphasize parenthetical expressions and to set off introductory series, appositives, and summaries. In typing, two unspaced hyphens indicate a dash.

EXAMPLES: 1. "Do you mean—can you really forgive me?" he asked. 2. "This apartment—it should be called a disaster area—needs raking out."

declension A listing of the various forms of a noun or pronoun, showing person, number, and case.

EXAMPLE: The complete declension of the relative pronouns:
Subjective: *who, which, that.*
Objective: *whom, which, that.*
Possessive: *whose, whose, of which.*

deductive reasoning The method of reasoning that begins with a generalization assumed to be true and which is widely accepted. That general statement is then applied to a specific case.

EXAMPLE: Most arguments based on deduction are actually extended syllogisms, such as the following:
  The reducing of taxes leads to inflation.
  This bill would lower taxes.
  Therefore this bill would lead to inflation.

See INDUCTIVE REASONING, SYLLOGISM

definite article The article that refers to a specific person, place, or thing.

EXAMPLES: *the* doctor (not *a* doctor), *the* street, *the* football.

degree, comparative The adjective or adverb form used to compare two things.

EXAMPLES: 1. He was the *larger* of the twins. 2. She moved *more gracefully* than he.

degree, superlative The adjective or adverb form used to compare three or more things.

EXAMPLES: 1. He is the *largest* player on the team. 2. She moves *most gracefully* of all the dancers.

demonstrative adjective An adjective that points out a noun or a pronoun and distinguishes it from others of the same class.

EXAMPLES: *this* book, *these* eggs.

demonstrative pronoun A pronoun that points out objects and distinguishes one from another without naming them.

EXAMPLES: *this*, *that*, *these*, *those*. "*These* are smaller than *those*."

denotation The direct, specific meaning of a word rather than its suggested meaning, or connotation.

EXAMPLES: The denotation of *Atlanta* is the city of that name; the denotation of *bridge* is a structure which carries a roadway over a depression, another roadway, or a river, etc. The denotation is the simple dictionary definition.

See CONNOTATION

dependent clause A clause that is subordinate to a main clause and which cannot stand alone.

EXAMPLES: 1. *When the bell rang*, the class was dismissed. 2. *After the class was over*, the discussion began.

descriptive essays Essays that are primarily detailed descriptions of a scene, a place, etc.

EXAMPLES: Topics that would make descriptive essays are "My Room," "The Decorations at the Junior-Senior Prom," and "My Butterfly Collection."

determiner A word that signals that a noun will follow.

EXAMPLES: The articles *a*, *an*, and *the*.

diagramming A traditional but now outdated method of placing sentence elements in a graphic organization to show their function in a sentence.

EXAMPLE:

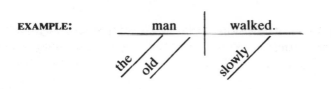

diction The choice of words in speaking and writing. Good diction requires the use of well-chosen words that convey the meanings and attitudes the writer intends and which are appropriate to the audience. Colloquial words are out of place in a formal situation, for example.

direct address A noun or pronoun, usually set off by commas in a sentence, used to indicate the person or persons being addressed; also called nominative of address.

EXAMPLES: 1. *Paula*, what happened to you? 2. As you see, *ladies*, we have a problem.

direct object A noun or another word or word group that receives the action of a transitive verb, a verbal, or a preposition.

EXAMPLES: 1. The punter kicked the *ball*. 2. We sat watching the *people*. 3. This treat is on *me*.

direct quotation A quotation in which the words of the speaker or writer are given *verbatim*, or word for word.

EXAMPLE: She said, "I will never leave this place." Indirect quotation: *She said she would never leave this place.*

double possessive Two possessive forms appearing in tandem.

EXAMPLE: John's father's car.

ellipsis marks Three spaced periods (. . .) that indicate parts of a quotation have been omitted. A fourth period is added when the omission is at the end of a sentence.

EXAMPLE: Four score and seven years ago our fathers brought forth . . . a new nation. . . .

elliptical clause A clause in which words have been omitted because the meaning of the sentence is clear without them.

EXAMPLE: My horse has been ridden every day of the week, but *his* [has been ridden] *only twice a week*.

emphasis Certain words or groups of words can be given emphasis (be made to stand out) by placing them at the end or at the beginning of a sentence, by inverting the normal order of a sentence, or by skillful repetition. The technique also can be used for making parts of a paragraph more prominent.

EXAMPLES: 1. I have only one word for him: No! 2. Him I do not like. 3. Go? Did he say "Go"?

ending The concluding section of a piece of writing. It is commonplace to say that an essay or story must have a beginning, a middle, and an end. The ending may be a summing up; however, it is often very brief, simply signaling the close.

EXAMPLE: So that is the way my summer went: slowly and painfully.

end punctuation Punctuation that comes at the end of a sentence. These include the period (.), question mark (?), and exclamation point (!).

exclamation point A punctuation mark (!) used after interjections, commands, and other emphatic statements.

EXAMPLES: 1. Go now! 2. Oh, no! 3. I will not leave now!

expletives Words that have the function of postponing the sentence subject.

EXAMPLES: 1. "*It* was on a midnight dreary." 2. "*There* is no end to the writing of books." The overuse of expletives can lead to a lack of emphasis and to a weak writing style. "Writing books is an endless activity" is the more conventional order.

expository essay An essay that explains or clarifies a subject.

EXAMPLE: Such an essay might have as a topic: "How to Cook a Turkey," "The Wars in the Middle East," or "How to Throw a Curve Ball."

fallacies Types of false reasoning or misleading arguments. Fallacies can make an argument weak and vulnerable.

See ARGUMENTUM AD HOMINEM; BEGGING THE QUESTION; GENERALIZATION, HASTY

false analogy A comparison, for the purpose of an argument, in which the similarity between the things compared is not significant in the essentials.

EXAMPLE: One might argue successfully that a government is analogous to a business; therefore, a successful businessman would make a good governor. A false analogy results if one argues that a government is like an elementary school; therefore a successful principal would make a good governor.

faulty coordination A type of error in sentence construction that occurs when there is no logical connection between two supposedly coordinated statements.

EXAMPLE: George was a ferocious dragon-slayer and was often seen musing beside a lake.

faulty predication An error in sentence structure that results when the subject and predicate do not fit together in meaning.

EXAMPLES: 1. *Faulty*: "A term paper is when you do some research and write it up." A sentence defining a term requires nouns in both the subject and complement positions; a clause beginning with *when* should not be used as a subject complement. *Better*: "A term paper is the product of research and writing." 2. *Faulty*: "A happy medium between a big city and a village would be a nice place to live." *Better*: "About midway between a big city and a village would be a nice place to live."

faulty subordination An error in sentence structure that results from the main idea being placed in a subordinate clause and a lesser idea in the main clause.

EXAMPLE: "Peter Rizzo was a freshman on the team,

although he was a better running back than anyone else." A correct way to state this sentence is: "Although Peter Rizzo was a freshman on the team, he was a better running back than anyone else."

figurative language A type of language that states or suggests comparisons between different ideas or different things. It is not meant to be taken literally.

EXAMPLES: Many examples of figurative language are so much a part of our everyday speech they are trite: "That math course is a *bad trip*." "I slept *like a log* last night." "*It's raining cats and dogs*." Better examples are found in literature, such as Stephen Crane's "He was naked, naked as a tree in winter, but a halo was about his head, and he shone like a saint."

figures of speech The two most commonly used figures of speech are similes and metaphors (*see Section I*); both are patterns of figurative language that compare things of different classes.

EXAMPLES: Metaphor: "She is a tigress when angry." Simile: "She is like a tigress when she is angry."

finite verb A verb that stands as the main verb of a sentence or clause. It can make an assertion or express a state of being.

EXAMPLES: "The diamond *lay* in the dusty road." Notice in the following that verbals, which look like verbs, are modifiers, not finite verbs: "The diamond *lying* in the dusty road was very valuable."

See VERBALS

footnotes Notes of reference, explanation, or comment placed below the text on a page or sometimes at the end of a chapter or book; usually marked with a superior number or an asterisk (*). The correct form for footnotes can be found in most English composition textbooks, such as Hopper, et al., *Essentials of English*, New York: Barron's Educational Series, 1982.

EXAMPLE: [1]John A. Giorgo, *Bridge Abutments* (New York: Technical Publishing Co., 1982), p. 306.

See BIBLIOGRAPHY

function word A word that indicates the relationship between other words in a sentence. Function words are articles (*the*, *a*, *an*), conjunctions (*and*, *but*, etc.), and prepositions (*for*, *of*, *in*, etc.).

fused sentences An error in sentence structure in which two sentences are joined (fused together) without a semicolon or without a comma and a coordinating conjunction.

EXAMPLE: "He had read the book he had seen the movie." A semicolon or a comma and the coordinating conjunction *and* are required between the words *book* and *he*.

See COORDINATING CONJUNCTION

future perfect tense The verb form that indicates an action will be completed in the future prior to another future action.

EXAMPLE: He *will have returned* before you leave on your trip.

future tense The verb form that indicates an action will take place later than the present; it is formed with the auxiliary *will* or *shall*.

EXAMPLES: 1. I *shall eat* spaghetti tonight. 2. She *will dine* alone.

gender The designation of nouns and pronouns as masculine, feminine, or neuter.

EXAMPLES: Masculine: *him*, *man*;
Feminine: *her*, *girl*;
Neuter: *it*, *car*.

generalization A pattern of logic in which one infers that what is true in many cases is true in all cases.

EXAMPLE: After reading about numerous muggings and acts of violence in large cities at night, one could infer that it is generally dangerous to walk alone at night in a particular large city.

See DEDUCTIVE REASONING, SYLLOGISM

generalization, hasty A type of fallacious reasoning that results when a generalization is drawn from insufficient evidence.

EXAMPLE: After a rainy, three-day visit to Philadelphia, one would be making a hasty generalization to conclude that "it always rains in Philadelphia."

general-to-specific organization A method of organizing a paragraph or an essay by beginning with a general statement, or generalization, and then presenting specific points of evidence to support that general statement.

EXAMPLE: One might use this method of organization in an essay beginning: "Big-city streets are dangerous at night."

genitive case The noun or pronoun form that indicates possession.

EXAMPLES: Noun: "*Bob's* book," "the *General's* car"; Pronoun: "*his* book," "that is *hers*."

gerund A verbal that functions as a noun and has an *ing* suffix.

EXAMPLES: 1. *Swimming* is good exercise. 2. I like *flying*.

See VERBALS

helping verb A verb form (also called an *auxiliary verb*) used with a main verb in a verb phrase. Helping verbs indicate tense and sometimes voice, person, number, or mood.

EXAMPLES: *will* run, *has been* seen, *could* go.

See AUXILIARY VERB

homonyms Words that are spelled and pronounced alike but have different meanings.

EXAMPLES: *Pool* in "swimming *pool*" and in "*pool* table"; *bowl* as in "rice *bowl*" and in "I like to *bowl*."

hyphen A punctuation mark (-) used either to divide a word at the end of a line or to join elements of a compound word.

EXAMPLES: If the word *decimate* came at the end of a

line, *deci-* would appear at the end of the line and *mate* on the following one. Remember not to divide words if a single letter is left at the end of a line or if there are fewer than three letters to move to the next one. Examples of compound words are "up-to-date report," "three-fourths."

idiom A word, phrase, or expression that is peculiar to a language and difficult to translate. Idioms are often not meant to be taken literally.

EXAMPLE: He is a *dark horse* in the Governor's race.

ignoring the question An attempt to gain agreement with one's argument by appealing to emotions like pity and fear while avoiding the real question.

EXAMPLE: "Because he is a lonely old man without friends and relatives, he should not have to pay taxes." This statement ignores questions relating to the man's financial condition and whether the government has the power to waive taxes at will.

illustration A method of organizing and developing a paragraph or an essay through the use of examples, anecdotes, and other means to support a general statement or topic sentence.

EXAMPLE: A general statement like "There is a great deal of dishonesty in the classroom" can best be developed by examples and illustrations.

imperative mood The verb form that indicates the speaker is giving a command, giving directions, or making a request.

EXAMPLES: 1. Get on board. 2. Please call me a taxi.

imperative sentence A sentence that gives a direct command and which employs the indicative form of the verb.

EXAMPLES: 1. Shut the window, please. 2. Fill out the form and put it in the box.

indefinite article An article (or limiting word) that does not refer to a specific person or thing.

EXAMPLES: *a* dog, *an* apple.

indefinite pronoun One of a large number of words used as pronouns that do not express a definite number.

EXAMPLES: *all*, *everyone*, *nothing*, *somebody*.

independent clause A clause that can stand alone as a sentence; also called main clause or principal clause.

EXAMPLE: Although he was young, *Mozart understood musical theory*.

indicative mood The verb form that indicates a speaker is making a statement or asking a question.

EXAMPLES: 1. I am reading *War and Peace*. 2. Have you read *War and Peace*?

indirect object A noun, word, or word group acting as a noun that does not receive the action (as does a direct object) but indicates for or to whom something is done.

EXAMPLE: "I gave *Emily* the apple." *Apple* is the direct object and *Emily* is the indirect object.

indirect quotation The paraphrasing of a person's statement; not an exact quotation. Quotation marks are not used.

EXAMPLE: She said that she had decided not to apply for the job.

inductive reasoning The method of reasoning in which one begins with particulars and concludes with a generalization.

EXAMPLE: Surveys and polls can provide materials for inductive reasoning. If a random sample of 1,000 college students indicates that 70 percent favor the candidate from the Democratic Party, one could conclude that candidate will receive a majority of the votes of college-age students.

See DEDUCTIVE REASONING

infinitive The verb form found listed in the dictionary; the plain form of verbs. When this form is combined with the infinitive marker *to*, the infinitive becomes a verbal, which can function as a noun, adjective, or adverb.

EXAMPLES: *to go*, *to stay*, *to remain*.

See VERBALS

inflection The change in form that words undergo to indicate their function in a particular context. The inflection of nouns and pronouns is called declension; of verbs, conjugation; of adjectives and adverbs, comparison.

See COMPARISON, CONJUGATION, DECLENSION

intensifier A modifying word that makes the word it modifies more emphatic.

EXAMPLES: *awfully*, *highly*, *very*.

intensive pronoun A pronoun that emphasizes the subject noun or pronoun by repeating it in another form.

EXAMPLES: 1. He *himself* said it. 2. I *myself* have said it.

interjections Words that exclaim and command the reader or listener to give attention. They can be inserted into a sentence or can stand alone.

EXAMPLES: 1. *Wow! Hey!* 2. *Say!* Let's hear it for Oscar!

interrogative A word or statement that has the form or force of a question.

EXAMPLES: 1. What? 2. Do you really mean that?

interrogative adjective An adjective that limits a noun and focuses a question on it.

EXAMPLES: 1. *What* road is this? 2. *Whose* book is lying on the floor?

interrogative pronoun A pronoun used in a question to stand for the person or object being inquired about.

EXAMPLES: 1. *Who* is she?
2. *Which* is his?
3. *What* caused that?

intransitive verb A verb that does not require an object.

EXAMPLES: 1. The dog *died*. 2. She *blushed* prettily.

irregular verb A verb that does not form its past tenses and past participles by the addition of *d* or *ed* to the infinitive form.

EXAMPLES: *give*, *gave*, *given*; *go*, *went*, *gone*.

italics Printed type that slants to the right to distinguish it from upright Roman type used in texts. Italic type distinguishes or emphasizes titles of books or plays, movies, television and radio programs, and works of visual art, etc. In writing or typing, italics are indicated by underlining.

EXAMPLES: *War and Peace*, *Hamlet*, *All in the Family*.

jargon A type of highly specialized language, often technical, used by certain groups and often not understandable to outsiders. The term originally meant "unintelligible talk" and is now frequently used as a term of contempt by outsiders. Sir Arthur Quiller-Couch, the British literary critic, popularized the term to mean verbal fuzziness of various types.

EXAMPLES: *habeas corpus*, a legal term; *stand by to come about*, a sailing term.
Using high-sounding words like *facilitate* for *make easy* is also a type of jargon.

limiting adjective An adjective that restricts or limits the scope of a noun.

EXAMPLES: Possessive adjectives: *his*, *her*; Demonstrative adjectives: *these* people, *this* card; Interrogative adjectives: *what* day? *whose* money?

linking verb A verb that relates a subject to a complement.

EXAMPLES: Common linking verbs are the forms of *to be*: "She *is* kind"; verbs related to the senses: "She *looks* beautiful"; and *become* and *seem*: "She *seems* happy."
Remember that adjectives, not adverbs, follow linking verbs: "She feels *bad*" not "badly."

loose sentence A sentence that has its main clause and main idea at the beginning, with subordinate details coming at the end. Loose sentences are less emphatic than periodic sentences, which are just the opposite in form.

EXAMPLE: Henry showed great strength when he lifted the sacks of grain, placed them on the truck, and drove away.

See PERIODIC SENTENCE

main clause A principal clause, which can stand alone as a sentence.

EXAMPLE: "Although he was not a fast runner, *he made the football team as a tailback*." The italicized clause could stand alone.

See SUBORDINATE CLAUSE

mass nouns Nouns that name things not normally counted.

EXAMPLES: *water*, *grain*, *people*.

misplaced modifier A modifier not clearly related to the rest of the sentence because it is placed too far from the term it modifies so that its meaning is ambiguous.

EXAMPLES: "Joe threatened to strike her often." "The doctor told him that if he did not start a program of jogging within a year he would be dead." Does the patient have a year to begin jogging or will he be dead within a year if he doesn't? The meaning is clarified by moving the clause *he would be dead* to its proper place, after *jogging*.

mixed metaphor An incongruous combination of figures of speech that often results in an unintentionally ludicrous effect.

EXAMPLES: 1. When you boil it right down to brass tacks.... 2. This is an attempt by the Republicans to throw up a dust cloud when they know their ship is sinking.

modifier A word that limits or qualifies the meaning of another word or words. Modifiers consist of adjectives and adverbs and as word groups that act as adjectives and adverbs.

EXAMPLES: *little* difficulty, *badly* hurt, man *on the trapeze*, strong *as an ox*.

modal auxiliary A helping verb that indicates mood (possibility, willingness, necessity, etc.).

EXAMPLES: *may*, *might*, *can*, *could*, *must*, *ought*, *shall*, *should*, *will*, *would*.

mood The form of the verb that indicates the condition or nature of the expression.

EXAMPLES: The indicative mood is for making statements or asking questions: "He is ready." "Are you ready?"

The imperative mood is for giving commands: "Be ready!"

The subjunctive mood is for expressing a wish or a condition contrary to fact: "I wish I were King." "If I were you, I would go."

narrative essay A type of essay in which chronological order is maintained. Almost all essays—even expository ones—contain brief narratives or anecdotes as illustrations.

EXAMPLES: Topics like "My Summer at the Beach" or "A Day in the Life of a Park Ranger" lend themselves to the narrative form.

See EXPOSITORY ESSAY

neologism A new word or a new meaning given to an existing word.

EXAMPLES: *COBAL*, *FORTRAN*, *software*, *hardware*, *modem* (all related to computers).

nominative case, of pronouns The pronoun form that indicates it is to be used as the subject of a verb or a subject complement.

EXAMPLES: *I*, *he*, *she*, *they*, *it*.

nonfinite verb Another name for a verbal; a nonfinite verb can never function as the main verb in a sentence.

EXAMPLES: "*Jogging* can be a good physical conditioner" shows a verbal used as a noun. "*Burned* toast is inedible" shows a verbal used as an adjective.

nonrestrictive modifier A phrase or clause that modifies terms but does not limit or identify them. Nonrestrictive elements are always set off by commas.

EXAMPLES: 1. This low-priced airfare, *valid for only this month*, is a real bargain. 2. Food, *which we all must have*, is both necessary and pleasure-giving.

non sequitur A faulty inference in an argument that does not follow from the premise. A non sequitur sometimes results from an oversimplified reversal of a universally accepted generalization; it also denotes the fallacy of assuming an unproved cause.

EXAMPLES: Everyone agrees that "haste makes waste," but we cannot reverse it to "waste makes haste." The statement that it will be an unusually cold winter because hollyberries are abundant is another type of non sequitur.

nonstandard language Language that does not conform in idiom, choice of words, grammar, or pronunciation to usage generally accepted by educated native speakers of the language.

EXAMPLES: *ain't, don't never, alright*.

noun clause A word group that contains a subject and predicate and functions as a noun. These clauses are always dependent, or subordinate.

EXAMPLES: 1. He did not like *what he bought*. 2. *Where you go* is of no concern to me.

nouns Words that name persons, places, things, ideas, etc.

EXAMPLES: *arrow*, *Jonathan*, *Philadelphia*, *democracy*. The plural of most nouns is formed by adding *s* (*horses*, *cows*) or by adding *es* (*foxes*, *boxes*); some terms of Latin origin form plurals in other ways: *radius*, *radii* (also *radiuses*); *stadium*, *stadia*.

number The form of a verb, noun, pronoun, or demonstrative adverb that indicates whether it is singular or plural.

EXAMPLES: *man*, *men*; *he* or *she*, *they*; *this*, *these*; *goes*, *go*.

object A noun, word, or word group acting as a noun that functions as a direct object, indirect object, or the object of a preposition.

EXAMPLES: 1. Joan found *whatever it was you said you lost*. 2. She gave *Georgette* the book. 3. To *whom* am I speaking?

object complement An adjective or a noun or a word group acting as an adjective or noun that modifies or refers to a direct object.

EXAMPLES: 1. Make your children *happy*. 2. They elected me *captain* of the track team.

objective case The form of a noun or pronoun that indicates the word is functioning as the object of a verb, verbal, or preposition.

EXAMPLES: 1. We defeated *them*. 2. He included *me* in the program.

obsolete words Words that are no longer in current use and therefore are unlikely to be understood by everyone.

EXAMPLES: *yonder, yon, forsooth*.

organization The structure, or skeleton, of a piece of writing; a plan for presenting material in an orderly arrangement. The four most common patterns of organizing details in written composition are described in the categories listed below.

See CLASSIFICATION, COMPARISON, ILLUSTRATION, PROCESS

outline, paragraph An outline consisting of a summary sentence for each paragraph in the written composition; often numbered.

EXAMPLE: 1. Before beginning to learn how to fish for trout, one must shop for the correct equipment.
2. A good instruction book on trout fishing can acquaint the novice angler with the basic lore of the sport.
3. Actual instruction in a trout stream, with a demonstration by an experienced fisherman, is very important.

outline, sentence An outline consisting of complete sentences for all headings and subheadings.

EXAMPLE:
I. In World War I, men were more important than machines.
   A. In many actions battalions of men, many not fully armed, were marched against similar battalions from the other side.

      B.   Airplanes and armored vehicles were in their early developmental stages.
   II. In World War II, machines were more important than men.
      A.   Long-range bomber planes were the most important factor in winning the war.
      B.   Sophisticated surface ships and submarines, equipped with radar and sonar, were vital to our war effort.

outline, topic An outline that uses nouns, or a word or phrase used as a noun, and their modifiers for headings and subheadings.

EXAMPLE:

    I. The reservoir and its protection
      A.   The prohibition of bathing, boating, fishing, etc.
      B.   The patrols to prevent violations
   II. The water tower in the reservoir
      A.   Its underwater windows
      B.   The screens to filter the filth
      C.   The pumping of the water to the purifying station
  III. The purifying station with its huge tanks
      A.   The settling of impurities in the water
      B.   The use of chemicals to aid the settling process
      C.   The condition of the water at the end of this process

parallelism The structuring of coordinate elements in a sentence so that they are in the same grammatical form, noun matched with noun, verb with verb, etc.

EXAMPLES: *Correct*: "I like a baseball game *that has exciting action* and *that keeps me in suspense*." *Faulty*: "I like a baseball game that is exciting and that keeps me in suspense."

parentheses Punctuation marks ( ) used to enclose nonessential elements within a sentence.

EXAMPLES: 1. President Kennedy's assassination (a traumatic event for our nation) occurred just before Thanksgiving. 2. George Carl (cousin of Joseph Carl) was forever in trouble.

parenthetical elements Elements in a sentence that may aid the understanding but are not necessary for the sentence to be understood.

EXAMPLE: Minor digressions and explanatory material are parenthetical elements. "He was not very swift (really quite slow) and yet made the team."

participial phrase A group of related words with no subject or predicate that functions as an adjective, modifying a noun or pronoun.

EXAMPLE: The girl *smiling through her tears* has just been named Miss America.

participle A verbal used as an adjective. The present participle ends in *ing* (*running*, *smiling*) and the past participle ends in *d*, *ed*, *t*, *n*, *en* (*eaten*, *finished*).

EXAMPLES: The words *cut*, *grown*, *burned*, and *learned* are all past participles in the following lines:

*Cut is the branch that might have grown full
    straight,
And burned is Apollo's laurel bough,
That sometime grew within this learned
    man.*

    Marlowe, Faustus

passive voice The verb form that indicates the subject is being acted upon. Only transitive verbs can show voice.

EXAMPLES: 1. The flower pots *were brought* indoors out of the cold. 2. The pie *was eaten* with gusto.

See ACTIVE VOICE, TRANSITIVE VERB

past perfect tense The verb form that indicates the completion of an action before another, more recent action.

EXAMPLE: She *had gone* before Enrico returned.

past tense The verb form that indicates an action occurred in the past.

EXAMPLES: 1. She *spoke* slowly and softly. 2. He *left* quietly.

perfect infinitive A form of the infinitive that uses the word *have* and a past participle to indicate a completed action. The form is necessary after past conditionals such as *should have liked* and *would have been possible.*

EXAMPLE: Horace would have liked *to have worn* his blue jeans to the formal dance.

perfect tense The verb form, used with the auxiliaries *have* and *had*, that indicates a completed action.

EXAMPLES: Present perfect: "I *have read* it." Past perfect: "I *had read* it." Future perfect: "I *will have read* it."

period A punctuation mark (.) that signals the end of a declarative sentence; also used to close abbreviations.

periodic sentence A sentence in which the meaning is not complete until the end; usually following the pattern of a dependent clause preceding an independent clause. The purpose of the periodic sentence is to hold the reader's interest to the end, as well as to add suspense. A periodic sentence is the opposite of a loose sentence.

EXAMPLE: Because the other children were laughing and pointing at him, he ran away quickly.

See LOOSE SENTENCE

person The pronoun or verb form that shows whether the person who is the subject of the sentence is speaking, being spoken to, or being spoken about.

EXAMPLES: In the first person the subject speaks: "I am here." "We are here."
In the second person the subject is spoken to: "Are you going?"
In the third person the subject is spoken about: "She was here a moment ago."

personal pronoun A pronoun that refers to people and which can be distinguished by person, case, and number.

EXAMPLES: *I, we, my, mine, our, ours, me, us, you, your, they, them,* etc.

See CASE, NUMBER, PERSON

phrase A group of words that are related but that lack a subject or predicate, or both. A phrase can act as a single part of speech, with varying functions. Types include the verb phrase, prepositional phrase, infinitive phrase, participial phrase, gerund phrase, and absolute phrase.

See ABSOLUTE PHRASE, VERB PHRASE

plagiarism The act of presenting as one's own the ideas or words of another. Plagiarism most often occurs in a research paper when the writer does not identify the sources of his information through footnotes or references in the text.

See ACKNOWLEDGMENT OF SOURCES

plurals A class of grammatical forms used to indicate more than one person, place, or thing.

EXAMPLES: aunt*s*, church*es*, formul*ae*, *geese*, rad*ii*, sta-d*ia*, dat*a*.

possessive case The noun or pronoun form that indicates possession.

EXAMPLES: Noun: *Jerry's* dog, the *teacher's* chalk. Pronoun: *his* dog, the chalk is *hers*.

post hoc fallacy A fallacy that results from assuming that because one event follows another, it is caused by the first event. In Latin the fallacy is called *post hoc*, *ergo propter hoc*, which means: "After this, therefore because of this."

EXAMPLE: The coach wore his red socks, and we won the game. If he wears his red socks for every game, we will win.

predicate The part of a sentence that consists of a finite verb or compound verbs.

EXAMPLES: 1. "He *ran* a good race." 2. "She *lighted* the candles." 3. "Jack *fell* down and *broke* his crown" (two verbs functioning as a compound predicate).

predicate adjective An adjective separated from the word it modifies and which follows a form of the verb *to be* (*is*, *are*, etc.) or another linking verb (*seems*, *looks*, *feels*, etc.).

EXAMPLES: 1. "The sky is *clear*." 2. "She feels *bad*." Notice that *bad* is the correct modifier because it is a predicate adjective that follows the verb *feels* and because it modifies the pronoun *she*. "She feels *badly*," using an adverb, is incorrect.

predicate noun Another term for a noun complement, which is a single noun or a word group acting as a noun that follows a linking verb and modifies or refers to the subject.

EXAMPLES: 1. I am the *President*. 2. My wife is the *First Lady*.

prefix Letters that can be added to the front or to the root of a word and thus form a new one.

EXAMPLES: *pre* + *fix* = prefix; *dis* + *like* = dislike.

preposition A word that links pronouns and nouns, or word groups acting as nouns, to the rest of the sentence.

EXAMPLES: *in*, *after*, *over*, *between*, *under*, *at*, *for*, *about*, *beside*, *from*, *within*, etc.

prepositional phrase A phrase that contains a preposition, its object, and any modifiers. It can function as an adjective, adverb, or noun.

EXAMPLES: *in the deep jungle*, *of uncertain origin*, *out of business*.

present participle A verbal that indicates continuing action; used as an adjective, adverb, noun, or part of a verb phrase (but never as the main verb of a sentence or clause). It can indicate present, past, or future, despite its name.

EXAMPLES: 1. My head is *reeling*. 2. I like to watch the *passing* automobiles.

See VERBAL

present perfect tense The verb form that refers to a single action already completed. (The past perfect tense refers to one completed action preceding another completed action.)

EXAMPLES: 1. I *have read* it. 2. You *have seen* the movie.

present tense The verb form that indicates an action is occurring in the present.

EXAMPLES: 1. I *jog*. 2. You *run*.

principal clause The main clause of a complex sentence, grammatically complete and able to stand alone.

EXAMPLES: 1. If you agree, *I will send it to you.* 2. Although she hated it, *she sat through the entire concert.*

principal parts of verbs The three verb forms from which the various tenses are formed.

EXAMPLES: Infinitive (or plain form): *sit*, *stand*. Past tense: *sat*, *stood*. Past participle: *have sat*, *have stood*.

process A method of organizing and developing a paragraph or an essay by describing the sequence of operations and actions by which something is done or made.

EXAMPLES: An essay on "How Wine is Made" or "Canning Vegetables" could be developed by the process method.

progressive tense The verb tense, formed with the auxiliary verb *be*, that indicates continuing action.

EXAMPLES: 1. I *am breathing*. 2. You *are breathing*.

pronoun A word used in place of a noun or a noun phrase.

EXAMPLES: Personal pronouns: *I*, *it*, *he*; Reflexive pronouns: *myself*, *herself*; Relative pronouns: who, which; Demonstrative pronouns: *this*, *that*.

proper adjective An adjective derived from a proper noun and which is capitalized.

EXAMPLES: *American* citizen, *Miltonic* simile, *Platonic* love.

question mark A punctuation mark (?) placed at the end of a question.

EXAMPLES: Where is Sam? Who are you?

quotation marks Punctuation marks (" ") (called inverted commas in Great Britain) that indicate material quoted directly. Quotation marks are also used to indicate titles of poems and other short works.

EXAMPLES: 1. "Why," she asked, "are you so angry?" 2. "To a Skylark"; "The Tell-Tale Heart."

reciprocal pronoun A pronoun that shows a cross relationship or mutual action between units in a plural subject or complement.

EXAMPLES: 1. Be good to *one another*. 2. Exchange caps with *each other*.

reductive fallacy (also called **oversimplification**) A fallacy in which two events are presented in a cause-effect relationship even though the causes may be much more complex than presented and the events may have no relation to each other.

EXAMPLE: The better sports teams a college has, the worse its academic programs are.

See POST HOC FALLACY

redundant phrase A superfluous, repetitious, and wordy phrase.

EXAMPLE: "George Washington *was a person who* told

the truth." The italicized words are redundant and should be eliminated.

reference of pronoun   An antecedent of a pronoun is also called the reference of a pronoun, meaning the word to which the pronoun refers.

EXAMPLES: "The *boy* found *his* dog in the woods." *His* refers to *boy*. Faulty pronoun reference can occur when there is undue separation between the pronoun and its reference and when the reference is ambiguous. Ambiguous: "Everybody could see that he was a handsome little boy who looked closely." Clear: "Everybody who looked closely could see that he was a handsome little boy."

reflexive pronoun   A pronoun that refers to the subject of the sentence, or the clause or the verbal phrase in which it stands.

EXAMPLES: 1. Can you feed *yourselves*? 2. I think I've hurt *myself*.

regular verb   A verb that forms its past tense and past participle by adding *d* or *ed* to the plain infinitive.

EXAMPLES: *close*, *closed*, *closed*; *mix*, *mixed*, *mixed*.

relative pronoun   A pronoun that qualifies or modifies an expressed or implied antecedent.

EXAMPLES: *who, which, that*. "I like girls *who* like me." "He is the one *that* scored the touchdown."

restrictive element   An element that make the meaning of a sentence clear by modifying or limiting basic elements of the sentence.

EXAMPLE: "Students *who study hard* will succeed." The *italicized* words are restrictive and are not set off by commas. Not all students will succeed: only those who study hard.

rhetorical question A question raised by a speaker or writer for effect and not in anticipation of an answer from the audience.

EXAMPLE: If a political speaker, in the course of a campaign address, asked: "Why is the economy so bad?" he would not expect a lady in the front row to stand up and answer him.

run-on sentence A sentence that strings together a number of main clauses joined by coordinating conjunctions such as *but*, *and*, *for*.

EXAMPLE: "George went to the bookstore, and he bought the book, and he read it, and he liked it very much." Run-on sentences are corrected by subordinating some of the ideas: "When George went to the bookstore, etc."

semicolon A punctuation mark (;) used to separate main clauses not joined by a coordinating conjunction, to separate main clauses joined by a conjunctive adverb, and to separate main clauses that contain commas.

EXAMPLES: 1. I cannot make the trip; please send Mary. 2. I cannot go; therefore you must send Mary. 3. We will send Mary, the cost accountant; John, the purchasing agent; and Murray, the assistant manager.

sentence fragment An error in composition (and a serious one) caused by punctuating as a sentence a word group that cannot stand alone as a main clause.

EXAMPLES: 1. After he ate the sausage. 2. When all is said and done.

See MAIN CLAUSE

simple predicate The verb and/or its auxiliaries in a sentence.

EXAMPLES: 1. She *adjudicated* the dispute. 2. I *have seen* the light!

simple sentence A sentence with only one clause.

EXAMPLES: 1. He went to the art museum yesterday. 2. I cannot eat cucumbers.

simple subject The noun alone, not including modifiers.

EXAMPLE: Idle *hands* are the devil's workshop.

slang Substandard language made up of newly coined words or special meanings of older words. Some slang is meant to be understood only by special groups: teenagers, college students, rock music fans, etc.

EXAMPLES: *the max* (meaning the maximum); *dope*, meaning a stupid person; *nerd*, meaning a nondescript but unattractive person by current standards; *humongous*, meaning gigantic.

See JARGON

solecism A blunder in speech or writing that results

from an ungrammatical combination of words or the intrusion of an unacceptable form or usage.

EXAMPLES: *don't never*, *ain't*.

space order   A pattern for organizing a paragraph or an essay in which details are described in a spatial relationship: going from left to right, near details to far details, etc.

EXAMPLES: Space order can work well in a descriptive essay or paragraph on subjects such as "The Quadrangle at King's College, Cambridge" or "The View from My Window."

specific-to-general organization   A method of organizing a paragraph or an essay in which particulars and specific details (the evidence) are given first, followed by a concluding general statement.

EXAMPLE: Any argument using inductive reasoning can be organized in this way.

See INDUCTIVE REASONING

split infinitive   An error in which the infinitive sign *to* is separated from the plain form of the verb.

EXAMPLE: "He likes *to* swiftly *run* through the woods." This would be *better* as "He likes *to run* swiftly through the woods."

squinting modifier   An ambiguous modifier placed in such a position that it could modify either the word before or after it.

EXAMPLE: He *only* likes turnips.

See MISPLACED MODIFIER

subject complement An adjective or a noun (or words acting as adjectives or nouns) that follows a linking verb and modifies or refers to the subject.

EXAMPLES: 1. I became an *auto mechanic* after a try at cooking. 2. She is the *best*.

See PREDICATE ADJECTIVE, PREDICATE NOUN

subjective case The noun or pronoun form that indicates the word functions as the subject of a sentence; also called the *nominative* case.

EXAMPLES: 1. *I* am unhappy. 2. *She* is joyful.

subjunctive mood The verb form that indicates the speaker is expressing a wish, a condition contrary to fact, a recommendation, or a request.

EXAMPLES: 1. I wish I *were* King. 2. If I *were* King, I would rule wisely. 3. Would you recommend that I *be* King?

subordinate clause A clause dependent on the main clause in a sentence.

EXAMPLES: 1. *After I finish studying*, I will watch television. 2. *When he left*, he took the dog with him.

See MAIN CLAUSE

subordinating conjunction A linking word that joins sentence elements of unequal importance. These conjunctions usually join dependent clauses to main clauses.

EXAMPLES: *as*, *because*, *although*.
"He had to walk *because* the car would not start."

subordination The indication that certain elements of a sentence are of lesser rank or importance than others.

EXAMPLES: "*Although he was weary*, he finished the race." The weariness is subordinated to the more important point, the victory.

substantive A word or word group that functions in a sentence as a noun.

EXAMPLES: 1. *John* loves *Mary*. 2. He likes *whatever is served to him at dinner*.

suffix A sound or sequence of sounds added to the end of a word to give it a new meaning or inflection.

EXAMPLES: willing*ness*, berate*d*, with*out*.

superlative The adverb or adjective form that indicates a person, place, or thing exceeds all others to which it is being compared. The superlative form cannot be used with fewer than three terms.

EXAMPLES: *largest*, *most unsightly*.

See COMPARISON

syllogism A method of demonstrating the logic of an argument by beginning with a general statement (*major premise*), then identifying a member of that generality (*minor premise*), then reaching a *conclusion*.

EXAMPLE: Major premise: "All ripe pears are sweet."
Minor premise: "This is a ripe pear."
Conclusion: "This pear is sweet."

See DEDUCTIVE REASONING, GENERALIZATION

synonym A word that has the same or nearly the same meaning as another. It has been said that no two words in English have exactly the same meaning.

EXAMPLES: *honest, trustworthy*; *brave, courageous*.

synopsis An abstract, resume, summary, or condensed version of an argument or a written composition. A synopsis is similar to an outline in that it shows how the parts of a work relate to each other; however, it differs in that it is more comprehensive and usually in complete sentences.

EXAMPLE: A student is sometimes asked to give the synopsis of a book as a part of a book report.

syntax The branch of grammar that deals with the way words are put together to form phrases, clauses, and sentences. Of a sentence where the words and phrases do not fit together properly, one would say that the syntax is faulty.

tautology A term describing the use of unnecessary, redundant words in speech or writing. The result is often ludicrous, but repetition can sometimes be used for clarity and emphasis, particularly in oratory, with good effect.

EXAMPLES:

> 1. When more and more people are thrown out of work, unemployment results.
>
> *Coolidge*

> 2. He wrote an autobiography of his own life.

tense The verb form that indicates the time an action takes place in relation to the present.

EXAMPLE:
Present: I *know*, you *know*;
Past: I *knew*, you *knew*;
Future: I *will know*, you *will know*.

thesis sentence A sentence that states the controlling idea and purpose of an entire written composition. A thesis sentence should be unified, limited in scope so that it can be covered in the time and space one has, and specific: vague, ambiguous thesis sentences are ineffective.

EXAMPLE: Although the town I grew up in was small and little known, it was filled with friendly, neighborly people.

topic sentence A sentence that summarizes the central idea of a paragraph; it may be the first or the last sentence.

EXAMPLE: "Although Henry was basically a shy person, he did not seem shy on that bright October morning." One can develop the paragraph with an example or brief anecdote.

transitional expression A word or phrase placed at or near the beginning of a sentence to show a relationship with the previous sentence.

EXAMPLES: *after all*, *accordingly*, *therefore*, *again*, *also*, *moreover*.

transitional paragraph A short paragraph consisting of a sentence or two that serves to call the reader's attention to the change from one subject to another.

EXAMPLE: Surely by now we can come to a solid conclusion, an answer to this puzzle. No, there are still several questions to be discussed and answered.

transitive verb A verb that conveys action and which takes an object.

EXAMPLES: 1. He *tells* lies. 2. She *earns* money.

See INTRANSITIVE VERB

unity An essay is said to have unity if all its parts relate to the thesis sentence and also relate to each other. When one finds that a new direction is needed in an essay, the thesis sentence probably has not been inclusive enough.

See THESIS SENTENCE

verb The word or group of words that indicates what state of being the subject is in or what the subject is doing.

EXAMPLES: *is, are, race, lie, fell*.

See INTRANSITIVE VERB, TRANSITIVE VERB

verbals Verb forms used as nouns, adjectives, or adverbs.

EXAMPLES: 1. *Relaxing* is important. 2. I also like *exercising*. 3. The coffee was too hot *to drink*.

See GERUND, INFINITIVE

verb complement The object of a verb, either direct or indirect.

EXAMPLES: "Never give a *sucker* an even *break*."

Both italicized words are verb complements; *sucker* is the indirect object and *break* is the direct object.

verb phrase A verb form composed of more than one word. A verb phrase usually functions as the predicate of a sentence or clause.

EXAMPLES: 1. He says he *has had* enough. 2. She *has waited* long enough.

vocative

See DIRECT ADDRESS

voice of verb The verb form that indicates whether the subject is acting or being acted upon.

EXAMPLES:
Active voice: "He *wrote* a story."
Passive voice: "The story *was written* by him."

vowels Speech sounds created by the free passage of breath through the larynx and oral cavity. The letters corresponding to these sounds are *a*, *e*, *i*, *o*, *u*, and sometimes *y*.

See CONSONANTS

wordiness A lack of conciseness in writing caused by the use of filler phrases (*as far as I'm concerned*), all-purpose words (*factor*, *situation*, *type*), and unnecessary repetition.

EXAMPLE: As far as I'm concerned, it is not a factor in this situation that I am a Democrat or that I am not a Republican.

INDEX

abbreviation, 91
absolute phrase, 91
abstract noun, 91
abstract poetry, 3
Absurd, the, 3
accent, 3
acknowledgement of sources, 91-92
acronym, 92
acrostic, 4
act, 4
active voice, 92
adage, 4
adaptation, 4-5
address, direct, 112
addresses, in business letters, 92
adjective, 93
  attributive, 97
  clause, 93
  compound, 105
  coordinate, 108
  demonstrative, 110
  interrogative, 123
  limiting, 124-25
  participle, 132-33
  phrase, 93
  predicate, 136
  proper, 138-39
adverb, 93
  clause, 94
  conjunctive, 107
  phrase, 94
affective fallacy, 5
agreement, 94
Alexandrine, 5, 40
allegory, 5
alliteration, 6
alliterative verse, 6
allusion, 6
ambiguity, 6-7
ampersand, 94-95
anachronism, 7
anacrusis, 7

analogue, 7
analogy, 7-8, 95 false, 114-15
analysis, 95
analytical criticism, 8
anapest, 8
anecdote, 8
antagonist, 8
antecedent, 95
anticlimax, 8-9
antistrophe, 9
antithesis, 9
antonym, 95
aphorism, 9-10
apostrophe (character), 95-96
apostrophe (in literature), 10
apothegm, 10
appositive, 96
apprenticeship novel, 13
archaic words, 96
archaisms, 10
archetypal criticism, 10-11
argument, 11
argumentation, 96
argumentum ad hominem, 96
article, 96 definite, 110 indefinite, 123
attributive adjective, 97
autobiography, 12
auxiliary verb, 97, 119

balanced sentence, 97
ballad, 12
ballad stanza, 12, 68
baroque, 12-13
beast fable, 13
begging the question, 98
bibliography, 98
bildungsroman, 13
blank verse, 13
bombast, 14
brackets, 99
burlesque, 14

business letter, 99-100
  addresses in, 92

cacophony, 14
caesura, 15
canto, 15
capitalization, 100
caricature, 15
carpe diem, 15
case, 100; genitive, 119; objective, 129; possessive, 135; subjective, 144
catastrophe, 16
catharsis (katharsis), 16
cause and effect analysis, 100-101
central idea, 101
character, stock, 78
characterization, 16-17
chorus, 17
circumlocution, 101
classical tragedy, 17-18
classicism, 18
classification, 101
clause, 101-2
  adjective, 93; adverb, 94; dependent, 111; elliptical, 113; independent, 121; main, 125; noun, 128; principal, 138; subordinate, 144
cliches, 102
climax, 18
closed couplet, 18-19
closet drama, 19
coherence, 102
collective noun, 102
colloquialism, 102-3
colon, 103
comedy, 19; farce, 35; of manners, 19-20; of situation, 20; tragi-, 84
comic relief, 20
comma, 103